Scholarly Editing in the Computer Age

Peter L. Shillingsburg

Scholarly Editing
in the Computer Age

Theory and Practice

Third Edition

Ann Arbor
THE UNIVERSITY OF MICHIGAN PRESS

Copyright © by the University of Michigan 1996
All rights reserved
Published in the United States of America by
The University of Michigan Press
Manufactured in the United States of America
∞ Printed on acid-free paper

1999 1998 1997 1996   4 3 2 1

A CIP catalog record for this book is available from the British Library.

Library of Congress Cataloging-in-Publication Data

Shillingsburg, Peter L.
    Scholarly editing in the computer age : theory and practice /
Peter L. Shillingsburg. — 3rd ed.
        p.   cm. — (Editorial theory and literary criticism)
    Includes bibliographical references and index.
    ISBN 0-472-09600-1 (alk. paper). — ISBN 0-472-06600-5 (pbk. :
alk. paper)
    1. Editing. I. Title.
PN162.S45 1996
808′.027 — dc20
                                                            96-18342
                                                               CIP

Contents

Foreword

This book began as an occasional essay and ended up a classic. It was prompted by a methodological, ideological dispute over how best to represent authorial intention in complex documentary circumstances and became a reasoned, articulate, and comprehensive statement of the textual condition in general. It was formulated as a practical investigation of the editing of nineteenth-century British fiction and turned into a *vade mecum* for the editing and textual scholarship to be undertaken in the twenty-first century. While still faithful to its origins in the Thackeray Project, and still drawing many of its most pertinent examples and counterexamples from Thackeray, it has transcended period and genre to achieve the status of a standard and necessary volume in the reading of any scholar hoping to comprehend the textual universe.

As such, it can be placed on that very small bookshelf comprising the canon of textual scholarship, along with Fredson Bowers's *Textual and Literary Criticism*, Jerome J. McGann's *Critique of Modern Textual Criticism*, G. Thomas Tanselle's *Rationale of Textual Criticism*, and James Thorpe's *Principles of Textual Criticism*. And like these other books, Peter Shillingsburg's *Scholarly Editing in the Computer Age* (*SECA*) is frankly polemical, in the sense that it is driven by a passion for its subject and a determination to engage with alternative procedural and conceptual dispensations. But unlike the others on this small bookshelf, *SECA* is marked by a resistance to categorization; it is not easy to place Shillingsburg and his oeuvre (of which *SECA* is probably the best-known exhibit) in any permanent ideological niche. This resistance is, I believe, a sign of the pluralism espoused by its author, an encompassing view that, while dismissive of incompetence and impatient with ill-considered argument, can comment authoritatively on the various movements and critical choices available to the contemporary textual scholar. Is *SECA* "intentionalist"? Well, yes, but. Is *SECA* "historicist"? Well, yes, but. Is *SECA* "sociological"? Well, yes, but. The force of those cumulative "but"s is that the reader can never be sure that Shillingsburg's book has been safely placed into a niche. Indeed, the critical method of *SECA* might almost be summed up by the "yes, but" formula: the sensitive textuist will always be aware of the qualification, the demurral, the alternative; and this unease with the quick and easy response will translate into a similar dissatisfaction with claims for the definitive, the positivist, and the teleological. The *work* of textual scholarship will never be done, and it is intellectually proper (even exhilarating) that this should be so.

Of course, what this means is that the work of pluralistic chroniclers and commentators like Shillingsburg will also never be done. So, while the publisher of this edition of *SECA* might have wished that I could now pronounce that the book is "finished," my experience as a reader of the three "states" of *SECA* convinces me that this is not Shillingsburg's last word on the subject and that hopes for a *consummatum est* are at best premature. This edition of *SECA* is very different, in scope, coverage, and balance, from the previous two, and it does in effect make those earlier editions obsolete, except perhaps as archival records of their time.

For example, the concluding chapter on desktop publishing is not just more up-to-date than the comments on computer usage in the earlier editions, it is also the inevitable culmination of the combination of technological power and critical judgement espoused from the very beginnings of *SECA*. That desktop publishing has a chapter to itself in this new edition certainly reflects the cultural shift of the last few years toward a new cottage industry of textual and editorial production in which the text-producer (the "editor") has enormously increased power together with similarly enlarged responsibility. But the chapter on desktop publishing is also a rational, even an expected, adumbration of the basic organizational and rhetorical principles laid down in the first edition of *SECA*. It is not just that Shillingsburg can now comment on technological changes and opportunities; it is also that the desiderata initially laid down by the early editions of *SECA* have been fulfilled by these technological facts. Can we therefore say that Shillingsburg's original agenda has brought about the technology? Not directly, of course: despite his expertise on, and proselytizing for, computer usage, Shillingsburg and *SECA* have not single-handedly *caused* the technological revolution. But it is the intellectual climate created by his and others' pushing of the technology envelope (McGann's Rossetti project and Hoyt Duggan's *Piers Plowman* archive are two notable examples) that has made textual editors into perhaps the most technically knowledgeable and accomplished of contemporary scholars outside the hard sciences. Textual scholars are certainly more at ease with electronic text than are most of their colleagues in literary criticism or theory, and it is the efforts of Shillingsburg and the influence of *SECA* that are symptoms of this familiarity.

If the polymorphous intellectual scope of *SECA* has always been a sign of the book's *synchronic* dynamic, so the continually shifting features of the book's balance and topical range are testimony to its *diachronic* resilience. The other books on that small bookshelf are, for the most part, self-enclosed and conceptually fixed. Thus, when McGann reissued his *Critique* a decade after its first publication, he did not send me a revised text on which to construct my introduction, for the text remained basically untouched. Similarly, the paper reissue of Tanselle's *Rationale* maintained the textual integrity of the original hardback edition. Obviously, it is not that these distinguished textuists have stopped thinking and exploring: McGann's later collections (like the *Textual Condition* or *Black Riders*) have expanded his frame of reference and refined his intellectual argument; and Tanselle, while frequently (and quite justly) referring back to the *Rationale* as his most comprehensive statement on textuality, has continued to write persuasively on various other matters (for example, in his recent essay, "Publishing History and Other History" [*Studies in Bibliography* 48 (1995): 269–89] on the concepts of *fact* and *proof*). But the McGann *Critique* and the Tanselle *Rationale* are, if you will, "readerly" or *lisible* texts: their meaning and their cultural function are circumscribed by authorial empowerment. Indeed, as I pointed out in my introduction to the reissue of the *Critique*, one of the ironies engendered by this socialized view of textual meaning and authority has been the subsequent attempts of its author to restrain and counter nonauthorial misprisions of his text (in effect saying, "No, that is not it at all. That is not what I meant at all").

One of the "strong readers" McGann confronts in his later explications of the *Critique* is, by nice coincidence, Peter Shillingsburg in an earlier edition of *SECA*. McGann notes that Shillingsburg's argument that "Jerome McGann's social contract theory of works of literary art ... rejects the notion of final authorial intention as an operative factor in textual criticism" (*SECA* [1986], 31) is an example of a "puzzling charge" made against his *Critique*, a charge that the author of the *Critique* rejects ("What Is Critical Editing? *TEXT* 5 [1991]: 24). This struggle over the "meaning" of a text, even a text in textual criticism, is to my mind wonderfully emblematic of the interplay among author, text, and reader that both the *Critique* and *SECA* address. A quick collation of the passage in the 1986 *SECA* with the text in the current version reveals that Shillingsburg has retained the basic language of his critique of the *Critique*, but has modified his phrasing by inserting "dominant" before "operative." A critical edition of the passage might read: 36 18–20 Jerome . . . . criticism] 1986 *om.* dominant.

Would McGann now be satisfied that, with the addition of "dominant" in Shillingsburg's revised text, the statement on his attitudes to final authorial intention in the *Critique* is now substantially correct? If "Critical Editing" is again reissued (beyond its subsequent appearance in McGann's *Textual Condition*) will he therefore revise his estimation of Shillingsburg's charge in the light of the revised text of *SECA*? Or do both the 1986 *SECA* and the 1991 "Critical Editing" (together with the 1983 *Critique*, on which they both depend) occupy a specific historical moment that has already construed cultural meaning? If McGann does not revise his charge about Shillingsburg's charge, will such subsequent appearances of "Critical Editing" be as strong a misprision of Shillingsburg's (revised) intention and expression as was Shillingsburg's misprision of the *Critique*? Did Shillingsburg revise this passage between 1986 and 1995 in deliberate response to McGann's expressed concern? If not (or if Shillingsburg were to deny that his revision was solely based on McGann's article), would we be justified in claiming that Shillingsburg's recollection was mistaken? Depending on how we resolve that question, should we include the "dominant" in a final-intentions edition of the states of *SECA*, or could we argue that the word was added only in response to external pressure and did not represent pure authorial intention? Two brief phone calls could easily have provided me with positions on (if not actual answers to) these questions, but to do so would have foreclosed critical argument by a meretricious appeal to "authority," and I have resisted the temptation. After all, what can authors tell us that is not already in the text? Should we not be able to make inferences about authorial intention and about authorial interpretation without recourse to external documents or protestations? What if the author were mistaken about or misremembered either the original intention or the subsequent interpretation? By denying myself the gratification of privileged information, I have left my own critical text "writerly" or *sciptible,* just as I believe Shillingsburg's *SECA* to be "open" and reflexive.

Having an open text can be a liability, for writerly incursions like that of McGann may continually prevent any teleological resolution. If

Wordsworth's *Prelude*, as a poem recording the "growth of a poet's mind," could by very definition not be finished until after that mind had ceased operating, so Shillingsburg's *SECA*, recording the growth of a critic's worldview, may not be completely *lisible* or closed while the textual world and the critic's perceptions are still in flux. My game of a critical edition of *SECA* can be only that—a game.

Nonetheless, there are good and profitable reasons for reading a revised edition of *SECA* at this particular moment. While no reader should be under the illusion that what we now have is all that Shillingsburg will want to say on such subjects as intention, ontology, and expectation, the view from 1995 is stable enough for the current version of *SECA* to be read as an authoritative statement for its time. Indeed, since I have already suggested that the book lays down the principles under which scholarly editing might proceed in the next century, I might even dispute the author's diffident temporal apologia that "this book and today's editions will soon seem locked irretrievably in the fading twentieth century" (preface). I see it exerting considerable influence way into the next.

The organization, from theory to practice to practicalities, follows what I have frequently cited as the epistemological narrative of editing, the way that the physical properties of an edition will be the "manifestation and accommodation" of theoretical assumptions. I think it only honest (not to say self-evident) that Shillingsburg makes clear that the various alternative approaches he deals with in chapter 2 will result in differently presented textual material. The "accommodation" between practicalities and their conceptual momentum will be accomplished in differing "manifestations."

That Shillingsburg has always been alert to this connection between accommodation and manifestation can be seen if we return to the original motivation for *SECA*, that "ideological dispute" that I referred to earlier. The principles in this dispute are discussed in Shillingsburg's account of Thackeray's punctuation practices and the problem of copy-text for *Vanity Fair*. But his tact and delicacy forbid his naming names in this forum (though he has been more forthright elsewhere, as in his essay on editing for the special 1995 issue of *Studies in the Novel*, where he specifically notes that the conflict over *Vanity Fair* led him to write *SECA*). In the absence of an authorial *apologia pro vita sua*, let me provide the institutional and cultural context.

It was very much as a response to a specific provocation that *SECA* was first published in 1984 as one of the Occasional Papers of the English Department at the Australian Defence Forces Academy (ADFA) in Canberra.

Shillingsburg had long been known as a great proselytizer for computer use in scholarly editing: his program, Computer Assisted Scholarly Editing (CASE), was written to produce in seconds the complex record of variance with which scholarly editors must deal. He had long been the textual avatar of William Makepeace Thackeray and had been responsible for setting up the protocols for the multivolume edition of Thackeray's fiction. And he had developed a cordial institutional relation with the burgeoning editorial work at ADFA, which was later to spawn the Australian Scholarly Editions Centre, the Academy Editions Project of Australian Literature, and the Colonial Texts series. These three interests met in the circumstances of the first publication, for the book used Shillingsburg's experience in editing Thackeray for much of its substantive illustration, it pointed to both the precarious state of such "positivist" enterprises as scholarly editing in an age of computer technology (while showing how that technology could be used in the service of a more flexible view of the editorial mandate), and it was produced by, and in part directed to, the Australian connection.

But there was more to it than this easy confluence. Like all good critical writing, even (or especially) that produced by textual scholars, *SECA* is passionate, animated, argumentative, even contentious. Its author believes deeply in the thesis and purposes of his book, and those purposes arose from an institutional confrontation that gives the book a biting, rhetorical edge. In the case of *Vanity Fair* v. the MLA's Committee on Scholarly Editions (CSE), Shillingsburg himself occupied a very ironic position. As one of the most authoritative and influential members of the CSE, Shillingsburg was concerned with promoting the critical evaluation of scholarly editions and in awarding the coveted MLA "seal" of an "approved" edition to those volumes meeting the high standards of the Committee. As editor of Thackeray, he was responsible to his author to make his writing available in as reliable and authoritative a form as possible. Usually, there would be no disjunct between these two responsibilities, but, in the case of *Vanity Fair,* institutional principle and the editorial reconstruction of authoriality came into conflict. Since only a part (but a significant part) of the authorial manuscript of *Vanity Fair* had survived, Shillingsburg had decided to use this extant document as copy-text for part of the edition, but, by *force majeure,* to use another copy-text (the first edition) elsewhere.

Obviously, this dual copy-text resulted in inconsistent usage; it could hardly be otherwise. Which was to rule—the law of consistency of usage or the duty of representing the author *despite* the accidents of documentary survival? Would the concepts of "authority" and "reliability" appear to diminish if there were more than one paradigm by which to adjudicate them?

Could an edition (and an editor) with two differing practices be trusted? This test case affected more than just the "sealing" fate of *Vanity Fair:* it brought to a head such sorely contested issues as the probity and purpose of scholarly editing, the status of documentary evidence, and the expectations of a critical readership. No matter that the CSE had already confronted more or less the same circumstances in the California edition of *Huckleberry Finn,* for which only the second part of the manuscript was thought to have survived at the time the edition was sealed: the subsequent rediscovery of the first part of the manuscript then led to the California editors' undertaking to re-edit the text (just as, I have always assumed, Shillingsburg would undertake to re-edit *Vanity Fair* if the rest of that missing manuscript were to be found). No matter that the CSE eventually committed a *volte face* and after first refusing the MLA seal to Shillingsburg's edition, later recorded its approval of the editing. What did matter was that the contention, just like those surrounding the noisier and more public battles fought over Joyce's *Ulysses,* the Oxford Shakespeare, the Kane-Donaldson *Piers Plowman,* or the Cambridge *Sons and Lovers,* emphasized that editorial theory and practice were both a site for critical intervention, for reasoned (and sometimes unreasoned) argument, and were inevitably the result of a human interaction with the mute records of history, which invariably remain mute until they are given voice by responsible editors.

I have sometimes referred to this intervention as a "licensed ventriloquism," and emphasized the role of editor as vicarious fulfiller of an absent authoriality. But whether seen as ventriloquism or through some other, more dignified figure, the speaking of the intentions of another is obviously a phenomenologically fraught and powerful role, and critics like Shillingsburg have been consistent in their determination that both the power and the difficulty of editing should be laid before the reading public. And better that open-handed gesture, even if it should result in the confession "I don't know," than a editorial disappearing act, whereby the text appears to constitute itself through the purely mechanical implementation of objective principles of bibliographical and historical research.

The main operational symptom of the CSE affair was, I believe, a faith in a well-articulated pluralism over the siren song of any single school of editorial orthodoxy. Shillingsburg maintained then, and has continued to maintain, that it is the editorial deployment of argument rather than the faith in a specific for all documentary conditions that will establish scholarly editing as a respectable intellectual discipline rather than a refuge for those who prefer not to think too much on the event. As I have already suggested, that pluralism may mean that it is difficult to pin him down, to declare him as a tried and trusted supporter of this and only this approach. While he has written on several of the various editorial ideologies of the last couple of decades—Greg-Bowers eclecticism, McGann socialization, documentary editing—Shillingsburg remains an elusive figure, even through his editing practices. For these practices are not easily caught by a single formulation, but maintain a deft and flexible relationship with changing documentary conditions and the changing purposes of an edition.

What should the neophyte or experienced editor look to find in *SECA*? First, a generous and comprehensive view that creates a narrative synthesis for this moment in the ongoing evolution of our discipline. *SECA* is very much of its time without being constrained by intellectual parochialism. Thus, the new sections on electronic editions (chapter 14) and on critical editions (chapter 8) encapsulate the epistemological and practical opportunities and limitations in two still very contentious areas of textual work. The descriptions of the choices available for desktop publishing are the clearest and most helpful I have yet read (even though I am chastened to read that the current 800dpi resolution we have been using for the camera-ready copy of *TEXT* does not meet Shillingsburg's prescription that 1200dpi is the minimum acceptable resolution for typesetting: back to the drawing board). Anyone wanting a "quick fix" on computer typesetting and electronic editions can do no better than to read Shillingsburg's chapters 12 through 14, where the mysteries of TEI conformable SGML are transparently explained. The liabilities of technological accounts are that they are always out-of-date and incomplete; but my guess is that Shillingsburg's eminently pellucid survey of the implications of electronic publishing of scholarly texts will remain a standard for many years to come. Such insights as the recognition that electronic formulation of text combines the strictly "editorial" process with that of actual book production make this section not just a mine of practical information written by one of the most technically experienced of present-day editors, but also a continually provocative analysis of the conceptual and procedural changes initiated by the electronic medium. As a medievalist and historian of text, I particularly liked his formulation that electronic editions are still in their "incunabular" stage, a statement that emphasizes the revolutionary nature of the move from print to digital production just as print itself was a revolution from manuscript production.

The other two sections of the book are equally inviting and thought-provoking. Using the documentary, aesthetic, authorial, sociological, and bibliographic "orientations" that speak for both his pluralism and his ability to comprehend the field at large, Shillingsburg continually stresses that no "single text will satisfy the needs of all five orientations," linking this argument with a deft account of the "differences of desire" among editors and arguing that "no single approach is the right approach. Critics and scholars need texts for different purposes." This comprehensiveness and large purview do not, however, mean that the book and its author have no defined positions in the textual debate. Shillingsburg prefaces his general account with an insistence that he will "not pretend to be without a position—without a ground from which to argue," and this grounded conviction means that he can have hard but direct words to say for some approaches, for example, noting the "dangerous" qualities of the platonic ideal.

Inevitably, in a book with such a vast conceptual and procedural agenda, there will be some arguments that need qualification or further exemplification. Again using my fast-slipping medievalist credentials, I would hesitate before accepting Shillingsburg's contention that the "aesthetic principle restricts emendations to those appearing in authoritative sources," for the sort of aesthetic "deep editing" practiced by Kane and Donaldson on the text(s) of *Piers Plowman* pretty much rejects the entire concept of an "authoritative" source on purely aesthetic grounds. Typically, the editors will construct an "unauthoritative" reading (i.e., one not supported in any of the extant sources) because it fits their concept of the aesthetic requirements of the poem. This *modus operandi* for "scholarly" editing thus approaches the rationale for "commercial" editing, which elsewhere in *SECA* Shillingsburg has differentiated from a genuinely scholarly procedure. But it is precisely this ability to conjure up the provocative remark inviting an informed response that marks *SECA* as such a stimulating yet even-handed contribution to the scholarly literature. I have demurred with parts of Shillingsburg's account before (as, for example, in my comments on his invocation of a "feasible grammar" for clarifying utterance in a text—see my qualifications to this argument in *Theories of the Text*) and no doubt others will do so. But I also recognize that, for the purposes of this book, some of his formal analyses work better than mine would: so, for example, his *abstract* "orientations" for types of editing are much more amenable to the sort of conceptual analysis he proposes than the practical, result-oriented hierarchy of edition-types I illustrate in Appendix II of my *Textual Scholarship*, and which Shillingsburg cites as an alternative system.

These debates on form, on propriety, on result, and on probity, will assuredly continue as long as scholarly editing and textual scholarship are accorded the critical, speculative component that most contemporary textuists would now endorse. Shillingsburg's *SECA* is one of the most powerful exhibits our discipline has yet produced in the ongoing attempt to persuade scholars who are *not* textuists that this critical component is a *sine qua non*. As such, it is a valuable cultural as well as intellectual artifact, a major force in the contemporary campaign to have textual scholarship recognized as not a positivist and outworn embarrassment to the academy but instead as a paradigm for what Carlo Ginzburg has seen as the necessary "speculative margin" (*Clues, Myths, and the Historical Method* [Baltimore: Johns Hopkins University Press, 1986]: 107) in all humanistic critical activity.

And while Shillingsburg is a particularly illuminating commentator on some of the recent polemics in our field that have sometimes descended to the level of street-brawling (his account of the Gabler-Kidd debate over Joyce's *Ulysses* is by far the best succinct and fair-minded analysis of the terms of the contention as they relate to contemporary textual discourse), his own rhetorical manner is urbane, sophisticated, and critically acute rather than partisan and blood-letting. As he shrewdly notes of the Gabler-Kidd affair, "the function of debate should not be acrimonious, but to lead to a fuller understanding of the enterprise." Would that all recent contributors to textual argument had been able to make this pronouncement and to follow it in their own work.

David Greetham
City University of New York Graduate School

Preface to the Third Edition

The surprising charity with which readers and reviewers of the hundred-copy first edition in 1985 and the 1986 trade edition greeted this little book hardly prepared me for a request for another edition. I have re-intentionalized—to use a word inspired by Hershel Parker's criticism of some revisions—every sentence saved from the original, taking into account some reviewers' criticisms, the shifts in editorial theory, and new visions of electronic editions of the last ten years. There is one new chapter in each of these areas (8 and 14). Because specific advice about computer technology tends to obsolesce before publication, I have tried to focus on general principles and methods for getting timely advice. Time stands still for no editor; this book and today's editions will soon seem locked irretrievably in the fading twentieth century. So be it.

I wish to thank, in addition to those gracious souls acknowledged in the 1986 edition, George Bornstein, without whose interest this project would never have been reborn and whose suggestions have led to substantive improvements. I am very grateful to David Greetham whose generous foreword to this edition leads me to question his judgment. To reviewers of the previous edition I'm indebted for pointers to weaknesses needing work; I'm especially grateful to Tim William Machan for understanding so thoroughly what I was trying to do in this book. To Ian Lancashire, Jack Stillinger, Gary Stringer, and James West I owe additional suggestions—some of which I was unable or unwilling to follow, I'm sorry to admit. And to Susan Whitlock and her staff at the University of Michigan Press I owe thanks for encouragement, support, and efficient organization in developing this revised edition.

Introduction

I once heard a young man trying to distinguish between "editing" and "editing editing." All I learned from his effort is that editing means something different to almost everyone who uses the term. In my lazy fantasies I dream of becoming the kind of editor W. M. Thackeray describes in the preface to *Comic Tales*, an 1841 collection of several of his pseudonymously published short novels. The preface is written by Michaelangelo Titmarsh, a pen name Thackeray also used for one of the included stories. In part the preface reads as follows:

> A custom which the publishers have adopted of late cannot be too strongly praised, both by authors of high repute, and by writers of no repute at all—viz. the custom of causing the works of unknown literary characters to be "edited" by some person who is already a favourite with the public. The labour is not so difficult as at first may be supposed. A publisher writes—"My dear Sir, Enclosed is a draft on Messrs. So-and-so: will you edit Mr. What-d'ye-call-em's book?" The well-known author says—"My dear Sir,—I have to acknowledge the receipt of so much, and will edit the book with pleasure." And the book is published; and from that day until the end of the world the well-known author never hears of it again, except he has a mind to read it, when he orders it from the circulating library.

Later in the same preface he continues:

> When there came to be a question of republishing the tales in these volumes, the three authors, Major Gahagan, Mr. Fitzroy Yellowplush,

and myself, had a violent dispute upon the matter of editing; and at one time we talked of editing each other all round. The toss of a halfpenny, however, decided the question in my favour; and I shall be very glad, in a similar manner, to "edit" any works, of any author, on any subject, or in any language whatever.

Here are some other definitions of editing current in our own time: editing consists of collecting, selecting, and preparing texts for publication. Copyediting is the imposition of consistent conventions for spelling and punctuation—sometimes called house styling. Commercial editing is improvement in style and suggestions for changes in content as well as expression. Usually commercial editing includes copyediting. Newspaper editing consists of securing stories (often called "copy"), typing, and copyediting them—in short, producing readable copy, usually in haste.

Scholarly editing has several definitions as well: *academic editing* (this for lack of a better distinguishing name, or perhaps for lack of a more distinguished name) is the term I use for the work of an "editor" asked by a publisher to write an introduction for a reprint, said editor not necessarily taking part in the selection, correction, or proofreading of the new "edition"—one step above Thackeray's celebrity editor. *Critical editing* is a term with several meanings. It is a name that connotes intelligence, the exercise of critical faculties; hence, it is currently fashionable. Fredson Bowers used *critical edition* to mean a text that derives from more than one source text. In general that is what I mean by the term as well, but enough disagreement has developed over the terms *critical* and *scholarly* to warrant a further analysis (see chap. 8). *Scholarly editing* also has a positive connotation in some circles; it is used to describe any sort of edition prepared by a person claiming to be a scholar. I use the term to describe what I do. The term should be reserved for editorial efforts designed to make available for scholarly use works not ordinarily available or available only in corrupt or inadequate forms. Some scholarly editions contain critical texts; some do not. Some scholarly editions are the product of good scholarship; some are not. To define scholarly editing in these ways is to say little enough about it. The kind of editing I discuss here is aimed at making works available for scholarly use. But there are several notions of scholarly use and a variety of ideas about how to serve scholarly needs. Furthermore, any fulfillment of scholarly needs is limited by the time and money available to the editor.

Let us refine our idea of scholarly editing by approaching the subject a bit differently. The purpose of any edition determines what editorial principles will be followed. If the purpose is to make presentable, agreeable, and attractive a work of current interest or artistic merit or pretension, then the editor may well be considered a commercial editor, copyediting the text and altering it to accommodate the predilections of the supposed audience. This is not scholarly editing; it is entrepreneurship. As members of a laissez-faire society, we shall say nothing against entrepreneurship, but we need not therefore confuse one thing with another. Commercial editing is not scholarly editing; it is enterprise.

If, similarly, the purpose is to rejuvenate a dead or lost work, the editor might feel even more liberty to change the text—to become the author's collaborator and produce an adaptation. Both of these purposes are pursued with seriousness by editors and cannot be dismissed as illegitimate. Just before I resigned as chairman of the Committee on Scholarly Editions of the Modern Language Association of America (MLA), a man called me on the phone to ask advice about editing *Peter Pan*. It seems that the original version was rather risqué and violent, but bowdlerization had early improved its popular success. Now the editor wanted both to restore the work's pristine vulgarity (substantives?) and to modernize its presentation (accidentals?) to make a new, rejuvenated *Peter Pan*. He addressed me in my official MLA capacity; consequently, I was forced to see that his proposal was made in all seriousness as a scholarly edition, not merely as a commercial enterprise.

Editors pursuing such ends apparently think works of art consist primarily of their emotional and intellectual content, that is, their meaning and the experience a reader has of it. Historical forms of the text are of negligible importance to them, and authorial habits and idiosyncrasies of expression are harmless at best and mistakes to be corrected at worst.

I should like to use the name *scholarly edition* for editions that preserve or rescue a work of artistic, social, intellectual, or historical importance as an artifact.

The word *artifact* seems especially suitable here because it subsumes the ideas of artistic construct and historic relic. Seeing literary works of art as artifacts justifies book collecting, bibliography, historical criticism, and textual criticism. A work of literary art, however, is not an artifact like the Elgin Marbles or a *Venus de Milo*. Like those artifacts, books often contain texts flawed by external ravages not of the artist's doing. Unlike those statuary works, literary works are susceptible not only to preservation but also to restoration. A scholarly editor first determines what to preserve and then edits, or perhaps de-edits, the work and supplies the ancillary material that will make the work, if not understandable, at least more accessible as artifact and as message or experience.

I would like, then, to drop from discussion the editorial problems of rejuvenating works, regardless of how important they are in producing movies or plays or adaptations or translations. I would also like to drop from further consideration what I have called commercial editing and copy-editing, regardless of how large and insistent the market for modernized texts may be. That leaves us with *critical editing* and *scholarly editing*, which for some are synonyms and for others not.

Textual criticism is often understood as the art of examining literary texts to authenticate the words, their order, spelling, punctuation, and capitalization. Authenticated texts are generally thought to be reliable for reading and studying literary works. Thus, textual critics are valued because they serve the laudable function of providing authenticated texts.

It is questionable, however, whether authenticated texts are what critics or close students of works of art need. I suppose I wrote that sentence to be shocking or perhaps to provoke argument. Crackpot statements have ceased to shock us, though, and of bickering we have had enough. But the statement's foundation is simple to explain: if scholarly editing involves critical judgment, authentication is a critical activity. It follows that persons relying upon authenticated texts are relying, unquestioningly, on the critical judgment of other scholars—something scholars seldom do in other spheres of their activities. From time to time editing is admitted to be a subjective activity, and, if that is so, arguments may never cease. The fury of many arguments may abate when the arguers agree on the meaning of certain words or when they are induced to look again at the objects of their intense concern. It is with the hope that certain objects of editorial concern will be seen more clearly and that arguments may be waged more cogently and productively that I offer this essay, though I shall not pretend to be without a position—without a ground from which to argue—myself.

Discussions of differences in position and purpose in scholarly editing and of its subjectivity seem to focus on several general issues, and disagreements appear to stem as much from a misunderstanding of the "opposition" as they do from the need to promote a position or theory that the editor has found most satisfactory for a particular text or class of texts. Such satisfactions depend upon the specific nature of the texts involved, on the tastes, training, and inclinations of the editor himself, and on the economic factors bearing on his situation. Furthermore, many disputants have discovered, in specific textual problems, situations to which the traditional editorial dogmas do not seem properly applicable. While in far too many instances this can be a result of not understanding clearly how traditional principles can apply to a given case, often enough editors also encounter novel situations requiring new principles. The outstanding thing, however, is that such editors have almost always appealed to some apparently unarticulated "principle within" to determine the supposed inapplicability of the traditional principles. I imagine editors are able to do this because they undertake their work to fulfill fundamental needs as literary critics rather than to exercise editorial expertise they already possess. One more often meets a noneditor with a text that needs work than a trained editor in search of texts to be edited.

When editorial principles lead toward decisions that would thwart the perceived needs that initiated the editing task, an editor may regretfully knuckle under and do what is thought to be required, or the editor may balk. Gordon Haight regretted the loss of George Eliot's pure dialect forms in the manuscript of *The Mill on the Floss* because he followed a traditional principle he thought required him to choose a later printed text as copy-text and to accept Eliot's apparent desire to tone down the dialects.[1] Likewise, in an account of his editing of Charles Dickens's *Bleak House*, Sylvère Monod lamented that he was forced to accept what he thought was an inferior reading because a compositor had misread the manuscript and Dickens had corrected the proof without referring to the manuscript, creating a revision that was acceptable but lacked the deftness of the original. Monod did not feel justified in violating his editorial principle that called for incorporation of later authorial forms.[2] Of course, not every editor regretfully bows to a principle that stands in the way of desired action. An editor may refuse to submit, developing instead new principles that will allow emendations "known" or perhaps just "felt" to be right. Often the articulation of the new principles is weak, giving rise to new arguments, put-downs (even send-ups), and alternate proposals.

I have tried in part 1 to focus on the editorial concepts that seem to give rise to inadequately articulated "principles." I have tried to identify what it is that we want in editing that occasionally seems to run contrary to received editorial wisdom. In doing so, I have tried to allow for tastes, values, and inclinations differing from my own, insisting only that a spade be called a spade if it can be recognized as such and that we use names to reveal concepts sharply and not to blur them with subtle connotations of

---

1. Gordon Haight, ed., *The Mill on the Floss* (Oxford: Clarendon Press, 1980).
2. Sylvère Monod, "'Between Two Worlds': Editing Dickens," in *Editing Nineteenth-Century Texts*, ed. Jane Millgate (New York: Garland Press, 1978), 26.

approval or disapproval. I do not think editing is a science, nor do I think many editors undertake their onerous tasks for any reason other than love. But I do admire Housman's call for the application of thought to textual criticism.

The specific areas I focus on in part 1 are, first, the concept of authority, because it seems fundamental to the idea of "authoritative texts"; second, the concept of forms, because "art is the perfect union of form and content," and because editors have long argued about "accidental" forms; third, authorial intention, because it is a slippery subject about which we have reached no agreement, and because some of us wish never to hear of it again; fourth, the ontological status of literary works of art; fifth, the concept of authorial expectations, because it provides a means of relating authorial intention to the necessity of a mediating publisher; sixth, concepts of artistic closure, because we seem not to agree about when a work is finished; and, seventh, the concept of ideal text, because we are all trapped in "the textual situation." The eighth chapter deals with the controversy over what constitutes critical editing. Or, to summarize another way, chapters 1 and 2 attempt to parcel out the editorial territory among the principal editorial theorists and practitioners; chapters 3 through 5 elaborate the problems within the camp of "authorial" editors, showing how their problems are interesting but very different from those of other types of editors; and chapters 6 through 8 return to the broader questions debated in the field.

After exploring these areas of editorial concern, I try to show in part 2 how the different views of them influence selections of copy-text (or base text), how they influence an editor's emendation policy, and how they affect the arrangement and scope of the textual apparatus.

I explore in part 3 some practical problems facing all scholarly editors, regardless of the theories they follow, and outline ways in which computer technology has changed the production processes and formal presentations of scholarly editions. I describe a variety of software packages designed to help editors do their research more efficiently, others that are useful in producing printed editions, and others designed as presentation mediums for electronic editions.

I would like to think that this book pulls together practical information and illuminates some arguments that have developed in isolation from one another.

Part 1. Theory

Chapter One

Authority

A review of current concepts of textual authority will help identify a widespread problem in literary and textual criticism that needs clear exposition in order to allow critics and editors to assess the significance and consequences of their own positions. Of course, many readers have not thought much about texts as such; whatever is printed in the book they happen to have suffices. Indeed, at first blush reader response theory seems to lend intellectual status to the notion that whatever a text says is okay because the work of art becomes a work only in the act of reading. New trends in literary theory only began to have a noticeable effect on textual editing in the mid-1980s. In midcentury modern textual criticism gained support because the New Critics focused attention on the text itself, and textual critics tried to provide texts that would deserve the new scrutiny. Other trends in literary criticism have directed attention away from authority and authenticity that concern historical critics, focusing it instead on forms and structures deriving from the culture as a whole and from language itself rather than from the individual author. Concern for what the author did—or meant to do or meant to have done for him or meant to mean—has been treated as theological mumbo jumbo and hagiolatry.[1] Textual critics have

---

1. Morse Peckham, "Reflections on the Foundations of Textual Criticism," *Proof* 1 (1971): 123–24; Tom Davis, "The CEAA and Modern Textual Editing," *Library* 32 (1977): 64 n. 19. More sophisticated treatments of the issues involved can be found in David C. Greetham, "Textual and Literary Theory: Redrawing the Matrix," *Studies in Bibliography* 42 (1989): 1–24; and Michael Groden, "Contemporary Textual and Literary Theory," in *Representing Modernist Texts: Editing as Interpretation*, ed. George Bornstein (Ann Arbor: University of Michigan Press, 1991), 259–86. See also Jerome McGann's "Theories of Texts," *London Review*, 18 Feb. 1988, 20–21.

nevertheless continued a rearguard action, thinking (perhaps rightly) that their conservative position is pure or authentic and that "sane" criticism still rests first on authenticated texts, historically derived; critical theorists might someday return to basics and require purified texts. While I think much of what semiotics and reader response theory is concerned with is relevant to textual editing, there has been no stampede among critical theorists to adopt the historicists' concern for authenticated texts. Textual purity has not been an exciting concept to critics enthralled by the role of reader in the act of recreating the work of art.

It is good to remind ourselves here that a twentieth-century reader of a seventeenth-century work is not seeing the same thing that his seventeenth-century predecessor saw, for to the original readers the work was new. Certainly, the modern reader of a new old-spelling edition is seeing something different. One controversy in editorial and critical theory focuses on whether these discrepancies are to be overcome by the reader "becoming" like his predecessor, whether the text should be modernized into a twentieth-century equivalent toward which the twentieth-century reader can stand in a relation matching the original or whether the attempt to see the work as it was first seen should be given over to the pleasures of seeing the work as it has become, from where we stand, as we have become.

For years textual critics have concerned themselves with authorial intentions, while literary critics busied themselves with rejecting the intentional fallacy and with the death of the author. The author as initiator of discourse is showing new life, and renewed interest in social institutions has given the author further life as a member of a community producing works of art as social phenomena. Some sophisticated critics cautiously speak of grasping the author's intention while assuring us that the author is not in control of, or proprietor of, meaning.

If textual editors take into account what the literary critics have taught us about texts as verbal utterances in contexts and what the sociologists have taught us of texts as products of social environments and what psychologists have taught us of verbal behavior and creativity, then they will prepare editions that can be used in differing legitimate "scholarly" ways. In any case, they already know from experience that editions are judged by several different standards, being praised and condemned for the same work.

Critics who reject the intentional fallacy and have a healthy respect for history tend to think of texts as autonomous. One logical consequence of this attitude is to prefer texts with historical integrity, artifacts from the past meaning whatever the words on the page seem capable of meaning, regardless of any intending consciousness behind them. And yet there is no logical necessity in a preference for unedited texts, since, regardless of authorial intentions, the corrupting influence of scribes or careless printers may have marred a text that might be more "accurate" or more aesthetically pleasing in its original form. Then again, some may argue, the mediating agency of nonauthorial hands may have improved the work. One's aesthetic tastes and one's value for historical discreteness or for "authority" will determine the attitude one brings to the text.

Among scholarly editors of the mid-twentieth century the prevalent view has been that the work of art is the author's—that the artist has the right of revision and that publishers, editors, friends, and responding readers may influence the work legitimately only if the author approves. That the author wrote or approved a particular text is what most editors mean by "an authoritative text." And yet the words *authoritative* and *authorial* are not synonymous to everyone. Nor is everyone agreed on what constitutes authorial approval. Some would like to weed out of the text any influences brought to bear by publishers. This pursuit led James L. W. West and others to produce an all-Dreiser version of *Sister Carrie*;[2] it led to the notion of producing Thomas Wolfe's posthumous novels as virtual transcripts of the manuscripts;[3] it leads to the desire to restore the first section of *The Sun Also Rises*, which F. Scott Fitzgerald had persuaded Hemingway to cut; and it leads to appreciative reactions to William Faulkner's famous remarks to his interfering editors about *The Sound and the Fury* ("And don't make any more additions to the script, bud. I know you mean well, but so do I")[4] and *Go Down, Moses* ("Print as is without caps and stops unless put there by me").[5] Even those who insist on the autonomy of the author, however, do not agree about what that means: Hershel Parker holds that, after the creative process has stopped, an author stands in the same relationship to his work as any other editor. It is no longer his. From then on he is a meddler or editor or merchandiser.[6] Another position is rep-

---

2. Theodore Dreiser, *Sister Carrie* (Philadelphia: University of Pennsylvania Press, 1981).

3. Jerome McGann, *A Critique of Modern Textual Criticism* (Chicago: University of Chicago Press, 1983), 79.

4. Quoted in Michael Millgate, *The Literary Achievement of William Faulkner* (New York: Random House, 1966), 94.

5. Quoted from memory of an oral account by James B. Meriwether.

6. Hershel Parker, "The Determinacy of the Creative Process and the 'Authority' of the Author's Textual Decisions," *College Literature* 10 (Spring 1983): 102–3; revised for *Flawed Texts and Verbal Icons* (Evanston: Northwestern University Press, 1984), chap. 2.

resented by Fredson Bowers, who put no time limit on the author's right to revise but who distinguished (or tried to) between revisions undertaken for aesthetic reasons and those effected under duress from nonartistic influences. Thus, he chose as copy-text for Stephen Crane's *Maggie* the first edition because its accidentals lie nearest to the purely authorial forms of the lost manuscript, and he emended the text to reflect the "artistic revisions" of the Appleton publication but not the bowdlerizations imposed by the publisher.[7] Other eclectic amalgams of authorial versions have been defended. Malcolm Cowley's edition of Fitzgerald's *Tender Is the Night* prints the sections in a new order declared by Fitzgerald before his death to represent his final wishes for the book. And Cowley corrected many spelling errors and smoothed the punctuation.[8] Matthew Bruccoli agrees that the spelling should be corrected but defends Fitzgerald's punctuation.[9] The least inhibited editors who hold for authorial autonomy produce editions in which all or most of the words are (to the best of our knowledge) authorial but which incorporate readings from several versions selected on the basis of the editor's aesthetic values in his attempt to present the author's "best" text.

Another, older idea of authority has had a recent resurgence. It arises from the observation that many authorial manuscripts have a decidedly unfinished look and that many authors willingly enter into a relationship with an editor/publisher for the purpose of converting "unfinished" manuscripts into published works conforming to "what the author wished his public to have." Indeed, observing that all authors enter into a relationship with a publisher (graciously or not, cooperatively or not) in order to convert manuscripts into what the work of art must be before it reaches its readers, Jerome McGann concludes that the "socialization" of a work in the production process is an integral part of creating a work of art. Authority for a text, he asserts, resides in that author-publisher relationship, and so the authoritative text is the published text. While he does not hold rigidly to this position, he considers it more compelling than authorial intention in determining what the authoritative text should be.[10]

To summarize, if we are to speak of authoritative texts, it seems necessary to locate the authority that controls the text. Some think of the text

---

7. Fredson Bowers, ed., *Bowery Tales* (Charlottesville: University of Virginia Press, 1969).

8. Malcolm Cowley, ed., *Tender Is the Night* (New York: Scribner, 1951).

9. Matthew Bruccoli, *The Composition of Tender Is the Night* (Pittsburgh: University of Pittsburgh Press, 1963), 206.

10. McGann, *Critique of Modern Textual Criticism*, 41–42, 44, 54.

as belonging to the reader. Some think the text is autonomous—once existing, becoming inviolably a thing in itself. Some think the text belongs to the social institution that includes publishers and editors as well as the author. And others think of the text as belonging solely to the author. Of these last, some think the author retains authority as long as he lives and revises; others think authority resides with the author only as long as he is controlled by the coherent intention of active creativity but is lost to him when that control passes.

As diverse as these positions may seem—and they can produce tremendous differences in the editing of any given text—they all share one thing in common: each is a means by which the critic or editor can select or create a text of the work of art that excludes all or most other versions of the text from the category authoritative text. It is true that many editors, from more than one of the positions described here, speak of alternative authoritative texts, but what they most often mean is that authoritative forms have been preserved severally in more than one source text. It is usually then the editor's goal to mine the source authorities to create a single "most authoritative" text, preserving either the form of the work that the author wanted us to have, or should have wanted us to have, or the form that some other concept of authority leads us to believe we ought to have.

The basic assumption of all editors seems to be that normally the end product of composition can be and should be one text that best represents the work of art. Of course, everyone recognizes exceptions: the original versions of Henry James's novels and the New York edition, so thoroughly rewritten that no editor could produce eclectic texts (the apparatus would be "of questionable utility," says Tanselle);[11] the three well-known versions of Marianne Moore's "Poetry," ranging from three to thirty-three lines long; Wordsworth's two *Preludes*; Stephen Crane's two *Maggies*; Shakespeare's two *King Lears*; Whitman's three (or eight?) versions of *Leaves of Grass*. Not everyone draws the line in exactly the same place for works that are "actually two works" and for which we need two or more authoritative texts. But the business of editing (particularly since the beginning of the preservation of original manuscripts and revised editions) has been twofold: the elimination of error and the selection of the authoritative

---

11. G. Thomas Tanselle, "The Editorial Problem of Final Authorial Intention," *Studies in Bibliography* 29 (1976): 195. Hershel Parker, who would reject the revisions as nonauthoritative because they were undertaken by the author after he had lost authority over the works involved, is not an exception; he, too, seems to want one best text ("Multiple vs. Single-Copy Texts: Henry James as a Test Case," Society for Textual Scholarship convention, New York, Apr. 1985).

readings for the new text, which supersede all other authoritative alternatives. What selection is actually made depends almost entirely on where the editor locates or finds the textual authority by which he proceeds to purify the text.

There is more piety than wisdom, however, in the concept of "purity" of texts. It is important for critic and editor alike to see that authority is a concept about which there is legitimate disagreement and that it is not an inherent quality of works of art but is, instead, an attribute granted by the critic or editor and located variously or denied entirely depending on the critical orientation of the perceiver. This concept I explore further in the next chapter.

Chapter Two

Forms

Editing is, above all else, a matter of forms. The content, the substance, the meaning of the work of art, has been usually thought of as the preserve of authors and of critical interpreters. But the forms, the details of presentation, are often thought to be the responsibility of editors. This distinction is basic to W. W. Greg's influential rationale of copy-text. Greg sees the authority for "accidentals" as existing independently from the authority for "substantives" because compositors and editors have traditionally treated substantives and accidentals differently.

Forms are patterns. Violations of form are recognized as such because they break a pattern. Literary works of art exist in language, the patterns of which are extremely complex and allow for tremendous variation. Editors have traditionally recognized the need to train themselves in philology, grammar, orthography, paleography, generic forms, and other areas, in order to be prepared to recognize the difference between a variation in and a violation of form. They are also prepared to accept as tolerable apparent violations of recognized forms if they find evidence to indicate that these were deliberate, as is the case in parodies, satire, irony. But, even where no comprehendible effect is achieved, editors have argued that evidence of deliberate action by an author justifies the result. For example, editors used routinely to alter *Mne* in Blake's *The Book of Thel* to *the* in the phrase "The daughters of Mne Seraphim." But recently editors have argued for the retention of *Mne* on the grounds that it was clearly and deliberately put there by Blake when he engraved the plate from which it was printed.[1] On

---

1. See *The Complete Poetry and Prose of William Blake*, ed. David V. Erdman (Berkeley:

the other hand, the sentence in *Vanity Fair* describing what the auctioneer at the Sedley auction did when Dobbin denied having made a bid on Becky Sharp's drawing of Jos on an elephant contains what everyone would recognize as an error, though no one has provided a really satisfactory correction. The text says that the auctioneer "repeated his discomposure." The best emendation offered is that he "respected his discomposure," but in the absence of manuscript evidence one cannot justify *repeated*, as in Blake's case, on the grounds that it was deliberate.

Critics and editors have been quick to recognize and try to serve the demands of a great many formal orientations. But, when these conflict, priorities emerge whereby some forms are valued over others, some formal orientations prevail over others. Since the tastes and values of the editor help determine these priorities, disagreements among editors and critics over how a text should be edited seem inevitable.

By formal orientation I mean a perspective on forms that leads to the selection of one set of formal requirements over another. Often this selection derives from value judgments about what the particular edition in question should provide as the material upon which to exercise literary criticism (i.e., what the "authoritative" text is). The major formal orientations are documentary, aesthetic, authorial, sociological, and bibliographic. Each of these general orientations has subdivisions, which I shall explore only far enough to establish the category and to demonstrate its capacity for internal division. The effect on the readings preserved in an edition will be seen to derive, to a large extent, from the priority given to these orientations by the editor. The formal orientation either reveals where the editor has located "authority" or governs where he will locate it. It is difficult to tell which comes first.

Before elaborating on this five-part scheme, I should point out the difference between it and the traditional classifications of types of edition: type facsimile editions, diplomatic transcript editions, critical editions with inclusive text, eclectic clear-text editions with multiple apparatus, parallel text editions, old- and modern-spelling parallel text editions with commentary, genetic editions, critical and synoptic editions, and variorum editions.[2] While it will become clear that some of these types are more compatible

---

University of California Press, 1982), 3, 790. Note the lingering disagreement evident in Harold Bloom's commentary in the same edition, 895.

2. This list is from David Greetham's *Textual Scholarship: An Introduction* (New York: Garland Press, 1994), 383. Greetham supplies specific examples of each, which explains the qualifiers on some of these labels. Those qualifiers indicate, incidentally, that such a list could be extended significantly.

with one of the formal orientations I am developing in this chapter than with others, it will also become clear that a difference in orientation will make a difference in how each of these types might be constructed. So, rather than showing a variety of kinds of edition that can be constructed, this chapter attempts to sort out differing assumptions about the formal charater of texts in the abstract, which have such an effect on how editors do their work. It explains in large part why editing is not a mechanical art that would be done in the same way by everyone who undertook the work with care and "editorial expertise."

The *documentary* orientation (called the *historical* orientation in the first two editions of this book), is founded on a sense of the textual integrity of historical moments and physical forms. Without necessarily valuing early forms over later ones, the documentary orientation frowns on the mixture of readings from historically discrete texts. The documentary orientation is used to support diverse editorial principles. Some editors would insist that the integrity of each historical document be maintained rigidly. In the past they tend to support microfilm projects and facsimile editions; some now advocate electronic archives. Emendations of errors in a document may be tolerated, but attempts to create a text with the best elements from two historically distinct documents is considered unhistorical—a violation by the editor of the historical form. Some editors with a strong documentary orientation, however, do not accept this narrow documentary historicism.

Some editors would purge a historical document of forms introduced "nonauthoritatively" and restore the forms that would have existed in the historical document had it not been for the nonauthoritative agency. The result is something of a correction of history. The C. S. Peirce edition, for example, while not governed strictly by the documentary orientation, adopted the word *reinstate* for emendations that restore forms predating the copy-text.[3] This violation of history in the name of history may seem odd but is not unusual. Many followers of Greg and Bowers consider that they follow historical principles when they produce an edition of an author's "final intentions." Likewise, followers of Thorpe, Gaskell, and McGann appeal to historical integrity when they insist on the "actualizing" agency of publication. Editors consider themselves historians when they trace the history of composition and textual transmission and when they prepare historical collations.

---

3. Max H. Fisch, et al., eds., *The Writings of C. S. Peirce* (Bloomington: Indiana University Press, 1982).

Other deliberate violations of documentary historical forms (including those by Bowers and McGann) are supported by appeals to competing formal orientations that are seen to take priority over the historical, even if only in some limited way. For example, when a text is judged to be inappropriate in its documentary form for reproduction, as when Jerome McGann opines that a transcript of a Thomas Wolfe novel from the manuscript would not be a novel but would in fact present Wolfe's work "in a light that never was on land or sea,"[4] he is invoking a nonhistorical formal orientation. While at first it may appear that he is appealing to a generic formal orientation (they would not be novels), he is in fact appealing to a sociological orientation (all Wolfe's other novels are known as they were produced by the drastic and necessary mediation of an editor and publisher). I remember, too, an editor commenting to me on Peter Shaw's plea for an edition of Emerson's journals "just as he left them."[5] This editor suggested disdainfully that Shaw simply order up a set of microfilms—indicating that Shaw's request was hopelessly naive. While most scholarly editors have a genuine respect for historical documents, and though all "scholarly editors" appeal to "historical principles," few are strictly governed by the historical orientation.

In fact, most of the other formal orientations used in scholarly editing are appealed to in order to "correct" historical forms. Insofar as editorial work is designed to eliminate errors and "textual corruption," its purpose is to mitigate the "ravages" or the "accidents" of history.

Authority, for the historical orientation, usually resides in the historical document, warts and all.

The *aesthetic* orientation is, in some ways, the least "historical" alternative, which may explain why scholarly editors seldom appeal overtly to it as an editorial principle.[6] One of the older jokes in editing circles is the definition of the aesthetic principle: to search out those words that the editor either does not understand or does not like and replace them with words that he does. Nonetheless, a great many emendations are made on the basis of an aesthetic orientation. Editors generally appeal to it when they declare their objective to be the preparation of the "best" text of a work. Commercial editors, literary agents, and other merchandisers of literary works unashamedly adopt the aesthetic orientation when they "improve"

---

4. McGann, *Critique of Modern Textual Criticism*, 79.
5. Peter Shaw, "The American Heritage and Its Guardians," *American Scholar* 45 (1975–76): 751.
6. See, however, James Thorp's "The Aesthetics of Textual Criticism" (*Principles of Textual Criticism* [San Marino, Calif.: Huntington Library, 1972]).

the work of their authors. Aesthetics being primarily a matter of taste, of course, it is possible to label any editor's aesthetic orientation in any number of ways—some are crassly commercial, some are coterie eccentrics, some are critically naive, others politically correct,[7] and so on. The point is merely that an editorial concern for the "best" text, for whatever purpose, is always an appeal to an aesthetic orientation toward forms.

Scholarly editors who appeal to this orientation usually restrict their selection of forms to those already existing in historical documents, though most will provide nonhistorical forms in the place of readings that they consider to be erroneous in all surviving texts. Bowers tried hard to exercise this orientation within respectably defined limits when, in editing Stephen Crane's works, he produced eclectic texts, selecting from among the alterations the "artistic" revisions but rejecting the "nonartistic" ones imposed by the publisher.

Aesthetic forms or patterns used by scholarly editors can be divided into many categories. Stylistic strategies, generic forms, conventions for "accidentals," and "consistency" are a few. An editor who defends an emendation of a historical document by reference to the generic form to which the text belongs (be it sonnet, villanelle, short story, or play) is giving an aesthetic orientation precedence over the strictly historical. The violation of the generic pattern reveals for that editor a mistake in the historical document. Likewise, appeals to the needs of modern readers for language that follows the conventions to which those readers are accustomed is a preference for currently aesthetic over historical forms. An editor who makes alterations defended as being more consistent than the source text forms is imposing an aesthetic over a historical form.

Authority for the aesthetic orientation resides in a concept of *artistic* forms—either the author's, the editor's, or those fashionable at some time.

Before proceeding to a discussion of the authorial, sociological, bibliographic orientations, an example here might clarify these general remarks on the documentary and aesthetic. W. M. Thackeray's *Vanity Fair* survives in various historical forms. There is a manuscript for chapters 1 through 5 and 8 through 13; two manuscripts for chapter 6, one of which is augmented by proof slips from a now otherwise lost typesetting of the first manuscript. The first edition, issued first in monthly installments and then

---

7. A. S. Ash's preface explains how an edition called *The Original 1855 Edition of Leaves of Grass by Walt Whitman* (Santa Barbara, Calif.: Bandanna Books, 1992) has "been humanized where appropriate (i.e., **human** or **person** substituted for **man** when the context clearly indicates no sexual reference is intended)."

bound as a single volume, represents a second typesetting for number 1, but an original typesetting for the rest of the book. The first edition went through six printings during which about 350 alterations of text were introduced. Editions set from the first edition appeared in New York and Leipzig immediately after the London publication. A revised edition appeared in London five years after the first.

An editor following a documentary (or historical) orientation might decide to reprint the first edition on the grounds that it is the first document to exist in complete form or might choose the revised edition on the grounds that it was the source text for the greatest number of editions of the book, hence the most significant historically. Such an editor might then provide a facsimile of the manuscripts and fragments of proof as a documentary history of the text. Or readings from those documents might be provided in a historical collation. Documentary editors will not give top billing to what the author intended or to arguments about whether one text has more authoritative accidentals while another has more authoritative substantives. They are interested in documents, in relics from the past, and wish to treat them as unities.

An editor following an aesthetic orientation might also decide to represent the text of the first edition or the revised edition, but the grounds for the choice would be different. Rather than say it is the first historical document or the most influential one, the aesthetically oriented editor might say that the conventions of punctuation are most consistently carried out in the printed text or that the manuscript is "unfinished" because its punctuation is incomplete and erratic. Furthermore, the aesthetician might point out, the first edition contains revisions (improvements) not represented by the manuscript. The editor might reinstate manuscript readings that are considered superior to printed forms, on the grounds that the production process was faulty, resulting in the inferior forms. Likewise, such an editor might mine the revised edition for "improved" forms that would have, or at least should have, been incorporated in the earlier text but were not noticed and improved in time. The choice of copy-text and the emendations made can be seen to result from an aesthetic preference for forms found in various documents over forms with historical integrity derived from the fact that they are contained in a single document.

Both the *authorial* and the *sociological* orientations are more "historical" than the aesthetic. The authorial orientation usually leads to the selection of authorial forms over nonauthorial forms. The authorial orientation is probably the most important in our time, though it has been under challenge in critical circles for years. Most editorial principles that discuss authorial intentions, whether "original" or "final," reveal an authorial orientation. Phrases such as "the text the author wanted his readers to have," "the author's final intentions," the "artistic intentions," "the product of the creative process," or even "what the author did" reveal an authorial orientation.

Authority for the authorial orientation resides with the author, though editors do not agree on what that means. Chapter 3 ("Intention") is devoted entirely to debates of primary importance to the authorial orientation.

Some representatives of the *sociological* orientation seem to adopt the authorial orientation, for they, too, speak of "the text the author wanted the public to have." But, when they say these words, they mean that authors do not usually want the public to read a manuscript and therefore willingly enter into working agreements with publishers and editors—indeed, some employ wives, mistresses, and secretaries to help transform manuscripts into published forms for the public. In his edition of Oliver Goldsmith's *Poems and Plays* Tom Davis notes that, in the absence of a manuscript, the printed copy-text for a Goldsmith poem preserves (1) some of Goldsmith's light punctuation (which he finds fortunate); (2) some of Goldsmith's errors not caught and corrected by the compositor of the first edition (which he finds unfortunate); (3) much of the compositor's heavy punctuation (which he finds a mixed blessing because it corrects the faults in Goldsmith's punctuation and obscures the finesse of his light punctuation); and (4) all the compositor's errors (which he finds unfortunate).[8] In short, he wants some of Goldsmith's light punctuation, but he is unwilling to reject all the compositor's work simply because the manuscript forms are inadequate. And so he accepts some of the compositor's work and rejects the rest, but he does not go beyond the simple distinction between light and heavy punctuation to defend or explain his procedure.[9]

The sociological orientation is revealed when the help given the author is noted as a social phenomenon, of interest and importance in itself, and integral to the creative process. Social institutions, and perhaps the historical fact of collaborative production of literary works, take precedence over the author. Apologists for this orientation cite examples of works by more

---

8. Oliver Goldsmith, *Poems and Plays*, ed. Tom Davis (London: Dent, 1975), 239.

9. Davis does, however, make an extremely useful distinction between routine, housekeeping punctuation and significant, meaning-indicator punctuation in a review of editions formally approved by the Center for Editions of American Authors in *Library* 32 (1977): 66–68.

than one author or by "lost" authors of whom we can know nothing and of works that lie unfinished and for which it can be said the author never expressed or revealed "what he wanted his public to have." These examples are given to illustrate the difficulty of applying an authorial orientation in particular instances. The documentary orientation is not a sufficient editorial principle, the sociologist insists, because unfinished works require the "actualizing" agency of publishing that the author would have initiated had the work been finished.[10]

Authority for the sociological orientation resides in the institutional unit of author *and* publisher.

To return to the example of *Vanity Fair,* an editor following an aesthetic orientation might draw from all surviving historical documents the best text—perhaps even the text he thinks Thackeray would have thought to be the best text (authorial and aesthetic). A sociological orientation would lead one to choose a published text, perhaps even the revised edition, as copy-text because it has passed through the normal social process of becoming a printed work. An authorial orientation would lead to the choice of the manuscript as copy-text where it exists and of the first edition where there is no manuscript. One of several emendation processes would then be followed to produce a text incorporating some stage of authorial forms but devoid of errors and of unnecessary nonauthorial intervention. The end product would be said to conform to the author's original intentions, to his final intentions, or to some concept of what the author is thought to have wanted or expected.

Another way to look at these orientations, a way that may help us to see why they appeal to some editors but not to others, is to note the way they divide or unify the idea of authority. By locating authority in the documents, the documentary orientation allows one to unify texts materially or physically. A historically interesting document presents a text. An editor may not violate that text's integrity except to correct its *nonsignificant* or meaningless elements. Historical editors have a range of views about what are nonsignificant textual elements: some respect typographical or scribal errors; some correct spelling; some render punctuation conventionally, or at least consistently; some alter paragraphing. Editors form images of readers whom they wish to serve, and it is the editor's concept of the reader's

---

10. This position was articulated influentially in McGann's *Critique of Modern Textual Criticism* but has been qualified and elaborated by Jack Stillinger in *Multiple Authorship and the Myth of Solitary Genius* (Oxford: Oxford University Press, 1993); and in Donald Reiman's *The Study of Modern Manuscripts* (Baltimore: Johns Hopkins University Press, 1994), though in the latter work the documentary and sociological arguments are mixed indiscriminately.

critical approach that helps him determine what parts of the text are non-significant and therefore should be rendered smooth or unobtrusive. Regardless of the extent to which the editor "edits" the text, the historical view of authority for any one text is monolithic. Variant texts have their own historical integrity. Historical editors do not produce eclectic texts.

Similarly, sociological editing tends to locate authority in single texts. While recognizing that in the production of a collaborative social phenomenon not all contributions to the work are of equal quality, the sociological editor tends to look for the text representing either the best-coordinated social effort of book production (the author in symbiotic relation with publisher and editor) or the most significant source text for the social impact or reputation of the work—the text that made the work famous. When there is more than one such text for a work, the historical inclinations of the sociological editor will lead to a desire for two or more texts, each having its authority in the social event that produced it or in the social event it caused. Sociological editors, like historical editors, will not violate the social event the text represents. In its purest form this orientation requires texts as produced, warts and all, though, like the historians, some sociologists are willing, perhaps for the sake of art, to edit what they consider to be the nonsignificant elements of the text. The significant elements, which they will not emend, include not only the words and their order but also the forms imposed deliberately by the social contract of book production. Hence, publishers' house styling of punctuation, for example, may be valued rather than lamented, and the editor may feel impelled to carry out more stringently a styling that was imperfectly imposed by the publishing process. But, like historians, sociologists do not produce eclectic texts.

The *bibliographic orientation* can be seen as an extension of either the documentary or the sociological, but in the last few years interest in it has increased sufficiently to warrant its separate discription. Based in the bibliographical studies of D. F. McKenzie, this orientation enlarges the definition of text to include all aspects of the physical forms upon which the linguistic text is written.[11] This approach does not admit to any parts of the text or of the physical medium to be considered nonsignificant and therefore emendable. The texture of paper, the type font, the style and expense of binding, the color, the indications on the book of the type of marketing undertaken,

---

11. See, particularly D. F. McKenzie's *Oral Culture, Literacy, and Print in Early New Zealand: The Treaty of Waitangi* (Wellington: Victoria University Press, 1985) and *Bibliography and the Sociology of Texts* (London: British Library, 1987).

the price, the width of margins—in short, all aspects of the physical object that is the book that bear clues to its origins and destinations and social and literary pretentions—are text to the bibliographic orientation. It is impossible to imagine what editorial policy would be in strict keeping with the bibliographic orientation rigidly applied, but the insights of this orientation are frequently alluded to in proposals for digital image reproductions in electronic archives, for which the bibliographical appearance of originals from manuscripts through mass-market paperbacks could be incorporated in order to preserve the broadest possible sense of text, including linguistic and bibliographic codes.

The bibliographic orientation can be approached from two interesting angles. Jerome McGann in reviewing McKenzie's *Sociology of Bibliography* indicated the way in which investigating books as publishing events for which the bibliographic code augments and determines the linguistic code can enrich our understanding of the social, economic, and artistic elements of their production.[12] He illustrates the value of the approach in various ways in *The Textual Condition*[13] And very interesting investigations by George Bornstein of Yeats's publications and by C. Deirdre Phelps of William Cullen Bryant have shown the fruitfulness of the bibliographical approach to literary productions.[14]

Secondly, the bibliographical approach can be applied to scholarly editions themselves, examining their construction and production for clues about how editors and publishers expect these new, usually heavy (substantial and important?) tomes to establish not only the texts newly edited but the canonical value of the works thus presented. One can ask about the scholarly edition what is the meaning of the binding, the dust-wrapper, the height, thickness, and weight of the book, the paper stock, the width of margins, line spacing, and type fonts. One could ask what is the meaning of the publisher's imprint, the Modern language Association's seal of ap-

---

12. "A Theory of Texts," *London Review of Books,* 16 Feb. 1988, pp. 20–21.

13. *The Textual Condition* (Princeton: Princeton University Press, 1991). See Shef Roger's correction of McGann's account of the bibliographical and editorial implications of decorative Ts Ezra Pound's *Hugh Selwyn Mauberley* in *Studies in Bibliography* 49 (1996) [forthcoming].

14. George Bornstein, " 'It is myself that I remake': W. B. Yeats's Revisions in His Early Canon," in *Victorian Authors and their Works: Revision Motivations and Modes,* ed. Judith Kennedy (Athens: Ohio University Press, 1991), 44–56; C. Deirdre Phelps, "The Edition as Art Form: Social and Authorial Readings of William Cullen Bryant's Poems," *Text* 6 (1994), 249–85, and "The Edition as Art Form in Textual and Interpretive Criticism," *Text* 5 (1994), 61–75. Despite the titles of Phelps's work, she focuses on original editions, not the bibliographical implications of scholarly ones.

proval, the institutional affiliations of the editor and editorial board members. One can ask the meaning of the price, of the advertisement fliers. And one can query the significance of tables of contents, the listing of editorial board members, the acknowledgements, and most important the size and position of the textual apparatus, and the location of editorial and historical introductions. All these questions bear on the notions editors, publishers, and readers have about the status and significance of the edited work.[15] Regardless of the approach editors take to the works being edited, the resulting scholarly editions of the last thirty years have tended to reinforce a basic notion of each work as equivalent to one best text. The physical dressing of that text and the ancillary materials attached to it have been at least in part unconsciously designed to determine reader responses in favor of the edited text. To say so is to practice the bibliographic orientation.

Both the authorial and the aesthetic orientations allow the production of eclectic texts because the concept of authority in each is a divided one—though on different grounds. Editors pursuing authorial forms of the text locate the authority in the author and find the work preserved in holographs and in documents the author has proofread. Since what the sociologists call the publishing institution is usually seen by the authorial editor as an agency of outside intervention (necessary perhaps, but evil nonetheless), printed documents have a high probability of containing nonauthorial forms to be edited out. Authorial editors find evidence of an author's work preserved in various texts, and their duty is to construct a purified authorial text from multiple sources. Greg's rationale for copy-text is founded squarely on splitting authority for accidental forms from authority for substantives.

Because they locate authority in the author rather than in a document, authorial editors will usually produce an eclectic text when there is more than one authoritative source text. Authorial editors usually conceive of readers as persons wanting to know what the author wrote. The differences among authorial editors about what the text shall be result from the different ways they think of authors exercising their rights over the text, as I explained earlier—some granting the author the right as long as he lives; others seeing the right terminated when the creative impulse cools; others granting partial or qualified authority to the author for all time; still others seeing authority, as I tend to want to do, as progressing in defined stages through composition and revision, frequently producing a series of distinct versions of the work.

---

15. I've explored this idea at some length in "The Meanings of a Scholarly Edition," *Bulletin of the Bibliographical Society of Australia and New Zealand*, 13 (1989), 41–50.

Editors appealing to the aesthetic orientation also divide authority in several ways. Usually, they divide it between the author and themselves, but sometimes they will find in the production process another (trusted) editor or advisor with whom to share the right to influence the text. From the historical texts aesthetic editors will select the forms they think the author wanted and accepted or should have wanted and accepted. Depending on how much such editors respect historical forms, they will adhere to or alter the text, appealing to what they think the author's aesthetic principles were, or what they wish they had been, to correct textual "infelicities." The result is always a critical eclectic text.

Adherents of documentary, sociological, and bibliographic orientations frown on the authorial and aesthetic editors for violating historical documents, or failing to accept "actual" social phenomena. Authorial and aesthetic editors do not find the significance or integrity of historical or social texts compelling enough reasons to maintain texts that are corrupt or impure. These editorial positions are all internally coherent and viable, but no single text will satisfy the needs of all five.

I have described these orientations as though they were discrete and mutually exclusive, but in fact many textual editors are influenced by more than one and choose copy-texts and make emendations by reference to a mixture of these influences. Often the particular circumstances surrounding a textual problem will themselves indicate the relative importance of the various orientations. Having chosen the most appropriate orientation for the editing of a particular text, it is possible to prepare an apparatus that will make the edition useful to persons wishing that another orientation had been employed. (This is one of the most important points I wish to make, and I shall return to it.)

It might be worth remarking that fierce editorial debates between partisans of these basic positions have been waged for years outside the ken of the formalists, structuralists, semioticians, poststructuralists, deconstructionists, and reader response theoreticians most of whom seem to wage their own debates with equal intensity over original documents, cheap reprints, or scholarly editions. But while that may seem to suffice for structuralists busily sweeping away textual surfaces, it is clear that semiotic and reader response critics might profit from knowing what editors, who have traced composition, text transmission, and relations between publishers and authors, can tell us about the context that an author brings to utterance in the act of creating a work of art. Clearly, it makes a difference not only what particular text we are responding to but also what we know about the creation and provenance of that text. Consequently, it is not enough for any editor or critic, regardless of orientation, to think of the scholarly edition as "the right text" for critical study. Critics must understand the principles and orientation of the editor producing it. And yet it seems in practice that every editor, regardless of orientation, is bent on producing the "right" text for scholarly use. As diverse as the aims of each orientation seem to be, all except the documentary orientation have in common a basic, questionable, assumption about works of art: that the end product of composition can and should be one text representing what the author wanted or should have wanted. There are exceptions, of course, as I have already noted, but they are thought of as exceptions, oddities, out of the normal run of things.

Chapter Three

Intention

The authorial orientation in editing has been for thirty or more years the dominant one in American scholarly editing. It informed all the principles of the Center for Editions of American Authors (CEAA) and had as its two most articulate spokesmen Fredson Bowers and G. Thomas Tanselle. Even Hershel Parker, who sometimes wore a button proclaiming Greg's rationale to be irrational (or was it too rational?), is firmly committed to the authorial orientation. Within this school authorial intention has been a central, if controversial, concept. It has guided editors in their choice of copy-text and in their emendation principles, and it fills the literature accompanying scholarly editions. The concept of the author's final intentions is ancient, though its name and influence blossomed in the mid-twentieth century under the CEAA. Nevertheless, it is a concept most editors have been uncomfortable with and that they find easier to use in practice than to defend in argument. It has, furthermore, been the central issue on which the Greg/Bowers school of editing has been attacked both by structuralist and poststructuralist critics and by Jerome McGann's social contract theory of works of literary art.

McGann rejects the notion of final authorial intention as the dominant operative factor in textual criticism. He says it does not apply to works that have more than one completed legitimate form and that it does not apply to unfinished works. Further, he rejects the concept of authorial intention as the primary concern of editors because it tends to make the author the autonomous authority over texts. McGann proposes as a more realistic view the idea that works of literary art are "actual" only when produced through the mediating influence of publication. The nature of authorial intention is of less importance to him as an editorial concept than is the fact of publication and the relative clarity of printed texts (i.e., works of "actualized" art) over manuscripts (i.e., "potential" works of art). His is definitely a sociological orientation.

While McGann makes some interesting observations on behalf of sociological concerns, his arguments against the authorial orientation—in particular his attacks on Bowers's and Tanselle's argument—are badly marred by oversimplification.[1] Furthermore, he fails to note the role authorial intention plays in his own concept of the editorial problem, as I shall point out. This latter is an important failure, for, regardless of the importance and legitimacy one wishes to grant to or withhold from the influencing agency of secretaries, publishers, and responsive readers, works of literary art are not only initiated by an author but typically grow to fruition under the control of the author, whose original writing, revisions, and reactions to suggestions are usually filtered through his own consciousness. This commonsense conception of authoring explains, though it may not justify, the growth and prevalence of the authorial orientation in scholarly editing.

It has continued to be usual, therefore, in spite of the death of the author movement, to think of texts as the products of authorial intention. Yet critics of the concept find its apologists to be metaphysical, if not downright theological, in their discussion of intention. And, of course, there are important critics who continue to find intention irrelevant altogether.

The problems and responsibilities imposed by the medium in which literary art exists and the implications of the creative process as they impinge on editing and on our understanding of the nature of literary works of art have become a central issue in editorial theory.[2] But the role of intention and of agency are frequently confused or unclear in such discussions. What follows is an attempt to examine the goals of editing in the light of an understanding of how works of literary art are created.

Questions concerning authorial intention fall into two closely related categories: one for those about the nature and recoverability of intention

---

1. I have tried to dissect the arguments for the sociological approach in "An Inquiry into the Social Status of Texts and Modes of Textual Criticism," *Studies in Bibliography* 42 (1989): 55–79. See also G. Thomas Tanselle, "Textual Criticism and Literary Sociology," *Studies in Bibliography* 44 (1991): 83–143.

2. Hershel Parker's *Flawed Texts and Verbal Icons* (Northwestern University Press, 1984) focuses on creative processes; Jerome McGann's *The Textual Condition* (Princeton: Princeton University Press, 1991) and *Black Riders* (Princeton: Princeton University Press, 1993) focused on the medium of literature. See also C. Deirdre Phelps, "The Edition as Art Form: Social and Authorial Readings of William Cullen Bryant's *Poems*," *Text* 6 (1994): 249–85.

and the other for those about the ontological status of works of art that embody authorial intention. The latter category involves the definition of *work of art* and the nature of the materials containing the evidence of authorial intentions. Consequently, the present and the next chapter deal with two parts of a single idea.

Theorists have tended to think of authorial intention as having a single goal. They have tended to de-emphasize both the development of intention through stages, toward completion, on the one hand, and the change or contradiction of intentions, on the other. And, though most editors acknowledge in principle the inaccessibility of intention, they have tended to ignore in practice the logical consequences of that principle.

According to James D. Thorpe "the ideal of textual criticism is to present the text which the author intended."[3] Thorpe admits, of course, that "this ideal is unattainable in any final and complete and detailed sense," but this does not prevent him from believing that textual critics must make the effort anyway and that literary students should rely on the products of their vain endeavors.[4] Bowers held a similar position: "The recovery of the initial purity of an author's text and of any revision (insofar as this is possible from the preserved documents), and the preservation of this purity despite the usual corrupting process of reprint transmission, is the aim of textual criticism."[5] In the years since these statements appeared, these positions have been frequently restated and elaborated in the literature of critical editing. Tanselle, for example, holds not only that "editing of individual texts of a work or the preparation of a record of the variants in them is a valuable accomplishment" but that, though to "go a step further and to apply critical intelligence to the evaluation of those variants is, of course, to take the risk of making mistakes ... that risk is the price that must be paid for the possibility of obtaining a single text which represents, as closely as available evidence will allow, what the author wished his text to be."[6] The very language acknowledges the inaccessibility of intention: "risk," "possibility," "as closely as," "will allow," "what the author wished." Yet it is clearly assumed that the author wished his text to be a single thing.

So when an editor says, as Tanselle does, "In a scholarly edition ... the aim is to emend the selected text so that it conforms to the author's

---

3. Thorp, *Principles of Textual Criticism* (San Marino: Huntington Library, 1972), 50.

4. *Principles,* 79.

5. Fredson Bowers, "Textual Criticism," in *The Aims and Methods of Scholarship in Modern Languages and Literatures,* ed. James Thorpe (New York: Modern Language Association, 1970), 30.

6. G. Thomas Tanselle, "Problems and Accomplishments in the Editing of the Novel," *Studies in the Novel* 7 (Fall 1975): 331.

intention," two questions immediately arise: first, is intention recoverable? and, second, is intention one thing that a single edited text can be made to conform to?

The best discussions to date of the recoverability of intentions are by Morse Peckham and Tanselle.[7] Peckham points out that intention is inaccessible by virtue, first, of its subjectivity; second, of its historical distance; finally, of its fluctuating and temporal nature. In his summary statement Tanselle merely comments, "One can never fully attain such a goal (or know that one has attained it), but at least one can move toward it by applying informed judgment to the available evidence."[8] He does not, however, explain how we can know we are moving toward something if we cannot know the thing we are moving toward.

There is a way out of his dilemma, nevertheless, and it lies in an examination of our second question: is authorial intention one thing that a single text can be made to conform to? *Authorial intention* is a term easy to misconceive, for it is used to denote various things. It is easier to see the irrelevance or unacceptability in literary and textual criticism of some of these meanings than of others. For example, there can be an intention to be brilliant or successful, to write a novel or poem, or to convey an idea, emotion, or attitude. A single unwavering intention, if such were conceivable, at any of these levels might produce several alternative texts of more or less satisfaction to the author—the textual options are nearly limitless. Most critics would reserve their own right to an opinion about the success of such intentions.

In pursuit of any one of these intentions the artist may "intend" on another level to construct scenes and plot them in chapters or sections; his intention with regard to the particular arrangement of scenes is apt to fluctuate, and his construction of a given scene may pass through many stages. Simultaneously, his intention to convey a certain message or effect may or may not remain unchanged. Parker gives a complicated example when he shows how certain changes in the book form of Norman Mailer's *An American Dream* had apparently unintended effects. The new version is complicated, since it contains at least one new set of intentions but leaves unattended the results of what might be judged incomplete, if not ill-conceived,

7. Peckham, "Reflections on the Foundations of Modern Textual Editing," *Proof* 1 (1971): 122–55; G. Thomas Tanselle, "Greg's Theory of Copy-Text and the Editing of American Literature," *Studies in Bibliography* 28 (1975): 167–229, esp. 211–19; and Tanselle, "The Editorial Problem of Final Authorial Intention," *Studies in Bibliography* 29 (1976): 167–211.

8. G. Thomas Tanselle, "Recent Editorial Discussion and the Central Questions of Editing," *Studies in Bibliography* 34 (1981): 23–65.

revision. One might say that the intention to leave something unchanged was subverted by intentional changes in other passages, the relation going unnoticed by the author.[9] An author's intention to word the sentences in a paragraph designed (or intended) to convey a certain message/effect may be firm, while the words and sentences themselves may undergo revision. These various levels of intention are firm or unstable in no predictable or standard pattern.

But one level of intention stands apart from these others. An intention to record on paper, or in some other medium, a specific sequence of words and punctuation according to an acceptable or feasible grammar or relevant linguistic convention is specific and singular. Any alternative execution of words and punctuation (except perhaps those that correct scribal errors) represents an altered intention at that level. The author's intention to convey an idea is important to editors because they know authors often produce alternative texts in their pursuit of a single intention of that kind. But one must be careful to distinguish this level of intention from an intention to record a specific sequence of words. More than any other level of intention, the intention to put down a particular sequence of words and punctuation is recoverable. Yet, even when given the survival of manuscripts, three things stand in the way of absolute recoverability of this level of intention: scribal errors, "Freudian slips," and shorthand elisions. We can not know for sure what message or effect the author intended the words and punctuation to have. He may have intended the words to be totally misleading. That level of intention is available to us only inconclusively through criticism. Each time an author intends a particular sequence of words and punctuation, however, a single text representing that intention results, and therefore the writer's intention for letters, spaces, and punctuation in a manuscript are more immediately (but not absolutely) within our grasp. Even here every letter of every word and every point of punctuation is susceptible to scribal error, Freudian slip, or shorthand elision, and we can only infer which is which. Of course, most of the words and punctuation marks are accurate and reliable evidences of authorial intention. If they were not, the manuscript would be incoherent.

The editor/reader of a manuscript has several guides in his efforts to identify errors, slips, and elisions: philology, conventional grammar and

---

9. Hershel Parker, "Norman Mailer's Revision of the *Esquire* Version of *An American Dream* and the Aesthetic Problem of 'Built-in Unintentionality,'" *Bulletin of Research in the Humanities* 84 (Winter 1981): 405–30; revised and reprinted in *Flawed Texts and Verbal Icons* (Chicago: Northwestern University Press, 1984), chap. 7.

spelling, the implications of context, and the form of the manuscript. Honesty, if not modesty, should keep editors from claiming too much for the results of their efforts. The arguments for the reliability of textual meaning, even when convincingly made (as I think they are in E. D. Hirsch's *Validity in Interpretation,* for example), do not claim absolutely to recover either consciously or unconsciously intended meaning. But these arguments are based on the laws of syntax, philology, and context, which are observable in normal communications. The editor applying them to the far humbler task of identifying errors, slips, and elisions has a higher probability of success. The problematic passages are usually not difficult to isolate, and clues to the author's intention with regard to words and punctuation usually abound.

It seems to me useful to distinguish two fundamentally different concepts of intention: the intention to mean and the intention to do. If we look at what Michael Hancher has called "active intention," which he defines as "the act of meaning-something-by-the-finished-text," we see he is still not down to the level of intention that can be recovered in any way beyond speculative criticism.[10] Hancher seems to see intention as a single, overall, controlling idea applicable to the single finished text of the whole work. But authors conceive literary works of art in many ways—as a whole or bit by bit, at one time or over a span of time, in one concentrated effort or in several discrete efforts. Execution of a work of art on paper introduces its own set of complications, as does production for mass distribution. In the context of creative acts we might see the author—as we no doubt all have experienced in our own writing—intend to mean something, followed by the intention to express that meaning in verbal form, followed by the intention to do something (i.e., write down the signs for the verbal expression of the meaning intended). In the act of writing or later upon reflection, the author may discover a new meaning to mean, which is followed by a new intention to couch the meaning in a verbal expression, followed by the intention to do something (i.e., write down the signs for the verbal expression of the meaning intended).

The intention to *mean* is inconclusively recoverable through critical interpretation; the intention to *do* is, with the three exceptions noted, more

10. Michael Hancher, "Three Kinds of Intention," *Modern Language Notes* 87 (1972): 827–51, esp. 830. Tanselle and Parker have both commented on the schema of intention proposed by Hancher. Tanselle finds it useful ("Editorial Problem," 174–77), but Parker is right, I think, in faulting Hancher for not accounting for intention in the act of composition ("The Determinacy of the Creative Process and the 'Authority' of the Author's Textual Decisions," *College Literature* 10 [Spring 1983]: 102–3).

immediately recoverable from the signs written. The processes of doing and discovering new things to do is the part of the creative process about which the editor must try to be accurate. From this level of intention critics attempt to construct or reconstruct meaning, about which the editor's best hope is to be plausible. This view of intention seems to provide some firm ground. Still, one must acknowledge that, in composition, intentions are multiple, and "intentions to mean" are irrecoverable.

The need that brings editors to editing is not usually satisfied by identifying an array—even a neatly chronological array—of written symbols in a progression of acts of intention to write down verbal expressions.[11] Typically, editors are initially attracted to editorial projects by a sense of the inadequacy of existing texts. An editor's sense of the importance of "meaning" may not depend on whether it is the author's, the text's, or the reader's meaning. But no concept of artistic creativity—not even a belief in the divine afflatus—ignores the fact that texts were created through some intending consciousness or perhaps through several consciousnesses, as when two or more authors collaborate or when a work emerges from an oral tradition or when it passes through a "collaborative" editorial and production process. Editors and critics ignore the variation of text produced in the creative process to their own detriment. One must remember that the creative process is often long and fraught with all the difficulties of execution, entailing writing, typing, copying, typesetting, proofing, revising, and correcting. In editing "authenticated" texts, we are not, then, only concerned with distinguishing between what the author intended and what was done to his text by others either against his wishes or in addition to his wishes, or in fulfillment of his wishes, but we must face up to the fact that, given the nature of creativity and the duration of composition and revision, the author's intention itself is probably not one thing that can adequately be represented by a single or simple authenticated text.

From this point on, then, when I use the word *intention,* I mean the author's intention to do—to record a specific sequence of words and punctuation that he thinks verbalize his meaning (whether premeditated or newly discovered). It is this concept of authorial intention that drives editors and critics to continue to use the word *intention* when dealing with the authority inherent in the initiator of utterance or discourse. The corollary is that from here on I will not use *intention* to indicate the author's intended

---

11. See Chap. 8, "Critical Editions," for a discussion of variorum texts and electronic archives, which do present texts as arrays or sequences.

meaning—which, if not irrelevant to critical and editorial concerns, is in any case irrecoverable with certainty.

Before continuing, we should acknowledge briefly a third concept of authorial intention that seems to appear in nearly all scholarly editing, including McGann's. It is revealed when editors speak of "the text the author wished his audience to read" or "what the author wanted his text to be." This concept of intention differs from what the author intended his text to mean or what the author intended to do. It involves the idea of what the author wanted or expected others to do. The idea of shorthand elision can be stretched to include not only the abbreviation of *and* to ampersand (*&*) or *which* to *wh.* but all those aspects of text that the author "intended" or "expected" to have altered for him as part of the service of rendering the work into printed form. This is an important concept lying at the foundation of arguments for the sociological orientation put forth by Thorpe, Philip Gaskell, McGann, Donald Pizer, Donald Reiman—and by some editors within the authorial orientation as well. These arguments usually are given in behalf of choosing printed texts as base texts even when manuscripts survive but are sometimes also given as a reason for certain classes of emendations. I discuss the concept in detail in chapter 5 ("Expectations").

The next question is: what is the editor's goal and the critic's desire? A single authenticated text? Or the material needed to face the literary work of art? It is true that authors strive to present a single text to a public; they proofread and choose one variant over another or replace a word or sentence with a new one and do not intend to have both printed. Likewise, readers expect to receive one text—continuity and coherence being highly prized in literary works of art—though most critics are prepared to accept discontinuity as a possibly correct part of the reading experience from time to time. The difficulty authors experience in producing one text, however, and their willingness, even propensity, to replace a received text with a revised text should alert us to the fact that literary art is different in its nature from some other forms of art, such as sculpting and pottery, in which the artist's choices are final and variant forms can exist only through the destruction of earlier forms or the creation of entirely new forms. Yet our treatment of literary texts is often based on an analogy with those essentially different art forms. What we know of composition, creativity, and intention shows us that variant authorial forms of the work can tell us much about the work itself, whatever that is.

The scholarly editor usually arrives on the scene long after composition is over, after the evidence of revision in manuscripts and proofs has begun to disappear, after the author is dead. He sees material bits of paper and ink bearing specific symbolic marks in various physical forms that often do not agree. Editors used routinely to think that a text representing an ultimate intention is the goal of editing, but many now contend that such a goal ignores what we know of the fluctuation of intention and that literary works of art, unlike some other forms of art, cannot safely be treated as single end products. Critics, in short, should demand from editors something more than a single, simple authenticated text.

I am not the first to notice that intention is not always one thing that a single edited text can be made to conform to. Tanselle's recognition of this point is extraordinarily lucid: "Obviously many writers have different intentions at different times," he writes, but he goes on to say that "in such cases one must decide which version of a work one wishes to edit, for no critical text can reflect these multiple intentions simultaneously."[12] The practical difficulty of presenting multiple intentions in a book is seen as more important than the conceptual insight that multiple intentions are operative. Editors and readers are interested, and rightly so, in having a text that can provide a suitable initial reading experience of a work, uninterrupted by textual problems or external considerations. This desire accounts for the widespread preference for a clear-reading text of the "best" text (however that is defined). But editors and readers are also interested in texts that can be studied, analyzed, read in bits and pieces, for the purpose of extending the initial reading experience with a deeper understanding of the work of art. If the creative process is clearly understood and multiplicity of intention acknowledged, a single text may be inadequate—misleading, in fact. Variant readings representing revisions (other authorial intentions) are an important part of a reader's experience of the work. And, while variant readings may often be seen, on the one hand, as mere trial efforts discarded on the way toward final perfection or, on the other, as postcreative meddling, they need not be regarded, therefore, as insignificant curiosities rescued from the workshop floor.

Given an authorial orientation, the editor's job may not be primarily to establish a text reflecting the author's best or final intentions as the editor critically perceives and appreciates them but, rather, to prepare a text and record the historical development of the authorial forms of the work so that the reader can study the whole work—a clear text and the authorial variant forms. Only with this material can a reader arrive at an informed

---

12. Tanselle, "Recent Editorial Discussion," 62.

judgment about what the author's work of art is. Presenting information in an orderly form, not just establishing a single authenticated text, is the editorial function.

Given a documentary or sociological orientation, however, the clear-reading text of the edited work must reflect the authority adopted: the historical document or the product of the social event. But what we know of the whole process should be accessible to the user in ways that will make his approach to the work as a whole possible and precise. Rather than a simple historical collation, the source of each variant, insofar as it can be identified, should be given. And I do not mean just the source document; I mean the source agent (author, editor, compositor) and the source time, so that the components of the text (both the reading text and the variant texts) can be seen as a developing whole. Even the aesthetic orientation can produce such an edition, in which the aesthetician can show where the text has been flawed by accidents, outside pressures, or missed opportunities.

For study beyond an initial reading experience, an edition without scholarly apparatus is seriously limited. To conclude that the preliminary or postcreative versions of a work can, for practical purposes, be ignored, we must maintain the fiction that a work of art is monolithic, the product of a single, consistent, ever-improving intention culminating in a perfected end product. This is particularly difficult to do, since not everyone agrees on which version of a work is the finished one.

Unfortunately, the apparatuses of many scholarly editions are designed to support the single-text approach, mixing authorial with nonauthorial variants indistinguishably. Editors either underestimate critics' interests in *authorial* variants or overestimate their patience in ferreting out variant authorial forms from the nonauthorial documentary variants. Not all apparatuses in modern scholarly editions fall into this error, but enough do to influence readers and critics to ignore scholarly apparatuses as the tedious productions of pedants.

Editors with an authorial bent may wish to leave out entirely the nonauthorial elements dear to historical and sociological critics. Sociological and historical critics may wish to ignore the distinct sources of the component parts of the work. Either approach limits the edition's usefulness. But perhaps the most important limiting factor of all is the naive approach we make as critics to the texts we treat as works of art by (1) seeing a single text as adequate and (2) assuming that a standard or scholarly text is the right text, without careful regard for the orientation it represents.

My conclusions, then, about the nature and recoverability of intentions are, first, that intentions are multiple, not singular, and, second, that, given the existence of adequate documents, multiple "intentions to do" are immediate and contrete enough to give the careful editor firm ground for his work. The moral I draw at this point is that critics learn about the work as a whole by identifying the agents of change and by tracing the stages of intentions and production. For critics to be able to do that, editors should provide a chronological arrangement of variants distinguished sociologically, historically, and authorially. Furthermore, editors should account for the significance of the linguistic integrity of documentary forms and the implications of their bibliographic codes.

Chapter Four

Ontology

Editors have begun to speak of "the print era" in opposition to the "computer age." One could say that in the print era there was a tendency to dismiss the implications of multiple intentions because multiple texts were too expensive and difficult to deal with in print. There were other causes. Two very important ones are, first, that the dominant formal orientation toward texts held that the final aim of authorship and editing was a single best text of the work, and, second, perhaps a consequence of the first, it was generally assumed that agreement had been established about the meaning of the words *text, version,* and *work.* One still hears editors and critics speak of "the work itself," in an attempt, perhaps, to distinguish the clear-reading text from the apparatus. But "the work itself" is represented in some essential ways by the authoritative variants buried in the apparatus.

As in chapter 3, the following discussion is focused primarily on the assumptions, methods, and goals of the authorial orientation, but the ways in which other orientations differ will be pointed out. Furthermore, in chapter 8 the alternative language of the documentary, sociological, and bibliographic orientations will be canvassed.

An inquiry into the ontological status of works of art and a critical look at the vocabulary used to refer to works of art and to the sources of textual evidence might shed light on the basic task of editing by showing us more clearly what we are working with and what the possible aims of critical editing can be. Only then will we be able to judge what the proper aims of critical editing should be.

It is important for an editor to conceive of the object of his endeavors, the work of art, first, as the product of authorial intentions and, second, as an object in time and space (materials containing the evidence of authorial intentions). Intentions are invisible, but we call the books in our hands works of art. If the editor proposes to recapture authorial intentions, he must examine carefully the relationship between intention and the paper and ink. I attempt to reveal that relationship by examining the nature of works of literary art and the materials containing them, analyzing and naming the mental forms involved in the concept of a literary work of art and the parts of the evidence an editor has at his disposal in editing a work of art. The names I suggest are unimportant; the definitions distinguishing one kind of evidence from another, one conceptualization from another, are all-important. The terms I use are familiar, but the definitions are, I believe, more precise and more useful than those in current use. My desire is to describe the materials and the basic concepts, so that we can know more precisely what is happening when an editor "authenticates" a text. The goal of a particular editorial project can better be determined after a clear look at the relevant materials and the concepts with which we handle the materials.[1]

WORK

From the author's perspective a work is the product of the imagination. It is shaped variously, grows, is revised, changes, develops in the author's mind. The author's notes and drafts are aids to memory and imagination. As the work achieves completeness of form in the imagination (aided by notes and drafts), the written representation of it achieves not only a fullness but also a stasis or rigidity. The fullness is useful to the ongoing process of creation, but the stasis is not. Authorial intentions for the whole work—the message or impressions, the organization, or the particular sequence of words and punctuation—may change in some ways, while they remain constant in others. (This point is demonstrated several times over by Hershel Parker when, in the process of illustrating a different idea, he gives several instances in which the effect of an unrevised passage is changed radically when changes are made elsewhere in the text.)[2]

---

1. This chapter should be considered as a basic introduction designed to sort out the general issues involved. See also G. Thomas Tanselle's *A Rationale of Textual Criticism* (Philadelphia: University Pennsylvania Press, 1989); and my article "Text as Matter, Concept and Action," *Studies in Bibliography* 44 (1991): 31–82.

2. Hershel Parker, "The 'New Scholarship': Textual Evidence and Its Implications for Criticism, Literary Theory, and Aesthetics," *Studies in American Fiction* 9 (Autumn 1981):

From the editor's and reader's perspectives a work is represented more or less well and more or less completely by various physical forms, such as manuscripts, proofs, and books. These forms often are not textually identical. From the receiver's perspective a work is the imagined whole implied by all differing forms of a text that we conceive as representing a single literary creation—James's *Roderick Hudson,* for example, in all its variant forms.

A work, therefore, has no substantial existence. Nor is it a Platonic ideal, that is, one fixed ideal form. Morse Peckham underscores the idea that a work has existence only as a construct by calling it a "postulated work."[3] It is worth noting that this conclusion derives not from the notion that the work is "actualized" only in the act of reading but from the fact that physically and verbally variant forms are all taken as *representing* the work. The work is only partially represented by any one given printed or written form. The redundancy of its various printed and written forms gives a sense of unity that helps us to conceive of the range of forms as one work, but its variants suggest the haziness of its outlines. The total destruction of manuscript forms does not sharpen the outline of the work; it merely diminishes the available evidence. Parker and Henry Binder make the point graphically in discussing the cases of Melville's *Billy Budd, Sailor* and Twain's *Pudd'nhead Wilson.* They conclude, too tentatively, I think, that "we simply cannot read certain books unless we first study the surviving draft pages or manuscript: and we may have to face the possibility that certain problematical books for which such evidence does not survive may be ultimately unreadable, however earnestly we will, of necessity, continue to attempt to read them."[4]

It is dangerous to think of the work as a Platonic ideal that the author strove to represent in some final or best version of the work. While the text may be monolithic in some specific instances (in which only one copy survives or in which all surviving copies are identical), it cannot be assumed to be so always. Many editors pursuing the author's final intentions fall into this way of thinking, and most literary critics, more is the pity, buy the argument. There is a pleasing simplicity in the notion that texts grow or

---

181–97; these and other examples appear also in *Flawed Texts and Verbal Icons* (Chicago: Northwestern University Press, 1984), *passim.*

3. Peckham, "Reflections on the Foundations of Textual Criticism," *Proof* 1 (1971): 127.

4. Hershel Parker and Henry Binder, "Exigencies of Composition and Publication: *Billy Budd, Sailor* and *Pudd'nhead Wilson,*" *Nineteenth Century Fiction* 33 (June 1978): 131–43, esp. 142–43.

develop or are shaped toward a final form—rather like a potter shaping a vase on a wheel. But the analogy is misleading. A book does not come in final shape directly from the artist's hands like a vase. Furthermore, unlike the vase, many literary works of art are formed over a period of time and are sometimes subjected to revisions at separate times representing distinct acts of intention. Works, the products of shifting, developing, and sometimes contradictory intentions, like Blake's boy child in "The Mental Traveller," cannot be nailed to a rock, made rigid and controlled, without destroying something.

VERSION

A version is one specific form of the work—the one the author intended at some particular moment in time.[5] A version has no substantial existence, but it is represented more or less well or completely by a single text as found in a manuscript, proof, book, or some other written or printed form. In other words, a version is the ideal form of a work as it was intended at a single moment or period for the author. The temporal limits included in this definition acknowledge the fluctuating intentions attending creative acts. For example, the ideal form of the work as it was intended by the author at the time of first publication may constitute one version, and its form at the time of the final revised publication may represent another version. Likewise, the version of a short story or play intended for public reading or performance might be different from the version of the same work intended for publication. A version has historical limits, even though these limits may be recognizable only in approximate ways. In order to proceed at all, the editor on the basis of manuscript evidence and biographical information posits historical periods in which it is conceivable that the author's writing was informed by a single or at least a coherent overall intention. For instance, the manuscript may represent the version produced in the

_____

5. The word *version* is sometimes used to mean the same thing as *book* or *edition*, each variant physical form of the work representing a distinct "version." It seems the waste of a good word to use it that way, but Jack Stillinger, for example, deliberately used it so, in order both to emphasize his rejection of the possibility of positing any authorial versions not represented by a document and in order that anybody could "look at the materials and verify that these versions do in fact exist" (*Coleridge and Textual Instability: The Multiple Versions of the Major Poems* [Oxford University Press, 1994], 118). For theorists such as Jerome McGann and Donald Reiman each production constitutes a new version in addition, because the meaning of each new physical embodiment of the work is defined to include the ways in which it indexes the economics of the marketing and reception of literary works of art. This position is further discussed in chap. 8, "Critical Editions."

heat of creativity, while the revised galleys may represent the author-edited version, and the final edition may represent the author's most mature intentions.

For reasons given already, this single overall intention (meaning or effect) is not recoverable, but the sequence of words and punctuation produced by the author at the time he was controlled by that intention is recoverable in the manuscript or in revisions. The version is the sequence of words and punctuation the author intended to put in readable form. The manuscript represents one version (or more if the cancelations are readable) and misrepresents the version only in scribal errors, Freudian slips, or shorthand elisions. Thus, the manuscript is not the version itself but contains a fairly accurate representation of it. The point is that, on the one hand, the work as a whole may consist of more than one coherent version and that, on the other, even the manuscript produced by the author may in some respects misrepresent the version it was intended to contain. I am trying to establish the concept of a work as fluctuating in its composition and multiple in its versions and to establish a distinction and a relationship between the work of art and the paper and ink we are accustomed to hold in our hands and treat as a work of art. Versions lack substantial reality, since the author's intentions may be imperfectly represented in any one written or printed text. Thus, even if a document embodied a version accurately, the version would remain insubstantial though substantiated because one could never know for sure—could never prove—that the version and the document were in that case coeval. Furthermore, a version may, be flawed or ill conceived; versions are ontologically ideal rather than real, but they are not necessarily ideal in the sense of perfection—not Platonic ideals.

DRAFT

A draft is a preliminary form of a version. Composition is often complex, sometimes tortured. Incomplete forms are often essayed by authors pursuing a coherent intention. Drafts of sentences, paragraphs, or scenes may be produced that cannot be thought of as belonging to completed versions of the work. Yet both critic and editor may well gather insight into the meaning or function of a version from acquaintance with false starts or experimental forms. Determining when a variant in a text is part of a draft and when it represents part of a new version may be difficult, but it is important to try to make that distinction, since one's response to a change may depend on whether it was produced by the same intentionality that produced its alternate form or whether sufficient time had passed to see the change as the product of a new effort. Drafts have the same ontological status as versions; they have no material existence. They are represented more or less well by the manuscripts containing them, but texts of drafts are also capable of misrepresenting the draft intention. As editors or critics, it is often easier to conceive of a draft for a part of the version rather than for a whole version. Drafts of whole versions are probably versions themselves. A version is a coherent whole form of the work as conceived and executed by the author within a limited time in pursuit of a reasonably coherent or constant overall intention. Drafts of parts usually precede the moment when the first version can be said to have been completed. And drafts of revisions may also precede subsequent versions. Again, the element of time is important to my definition. Variants (other than corrections of errors) produced at significant intervals of time belong to subsequent versions, rather than being drafts.

TEXT

A text is the actual order of words and punctuation as contained in any one physical form, such as manuscript, proof, or book. A text is the product of the author's, or the author-and-others', physical activity in the attempt to store in tangible form the version the author currently intends. And yet a text (the *order* of words and punctuation) has no substantial or material existence, since it is not restricted by time and space. That is, the same text can exist simultaneously in the memory, in more than one copy or in more than one form. The text is contained and stabilized by the physical form but is not the physical form itself. Each text represents more or less well or completely a version of the work. A manuscript may actually contain two or even more texts: that represented by the original reading including those portions now canceled and that represented by the final revision or that represented by intermediate readings.

The capacity of a printed or written *text* to misrepresent a *version* of the work lies in the capacity of writers and printers to commit scribal and Freudian errors and of printers, editors, and others to impose unauthorized "improvements" that may not correspond with the author's intention for the current version.

STORAGE MEDIUM

The conventions governing the relationships between the sequence of words and pauses—the text—and the linguistic signs that store the text (i.e., the letters and punctuation marks on the page) are so well established that it hardly seems profitable to distinguish between text and sign. Yet, it is possible for the same text to be stored in a set of alphabetical signs, a set of braille signs, a set of electronic signals on a computer tape, and a set of magnetic impulses on a tape recorder. Therefore, it is not accurate to say that the text and the signs or storage medium are the same. If the text is stored accurately on a second storage medium, the text remains the same though the signs for it are different. Each accurate copy contains the same text; inaccurate or otherwise variant copies contain new texts.

DOCUMENT

A document consists of the physical material, paper and ink, bearing the configuration of signs that represents a text. Documents have material existence. Each new copy of a text, whether accurate or inaccurate, is a new document.

The usefulness of this taxonomy for the materials of textual criticism lies in its clarification of the relationships between intangible irrecoverable intentions and the paper and ink we hold in our hands—a clarification important to readers as well as to editors. Now we can make clear statements about variants and their relationship to the historical texts containing them, the versions they represent, and the ways in which they constitute part of the intended work.

It is important to note that from this point on, when I say *work* or *version*, I refer to nonmaterial authorial intentions; when I say *text*, I refer to a sequence of words and punctuation found on a document. Texts may contain nonauthorial parts; versions do not.[6]

---

6. Again it is important to note that editorial theorists of the documentary, bibliographical, and sociological orientations frequently equate version with document and reject the idea of version and work, as defined here, because they are ideals. They prefer to work with what Stillinger calls "real texts: versions on paper" (*Coleridge*, 129). The net effect of their ideas is to prevent the editor of any newly edited text from extracting the work of one particular agent, say the author, from the multiplicity of variant documents. They have cogent reasons within their own editorial orientations for that, but, since they do not reflect the authorial orientation, their cavils cannot apply to the work of an editor who is.

The next crucial question for the editor who acknowledges the importance of variant versions is to decide which version of the work shall be represented by the clear-reading text and how the other authorial versions or textual forms will be presented in an apparatus or footnotes. The first conclusion is that no single version, whether historical or eclectic, is an adequate representation of the work for those students and readers who want more than an initial reading experience of the work.

Let us pause a moment to consider what this may mean to the other, nonauthorial orientations set out in chapter 2. The documentary orientation may seem unfazed by all this, because documents are what they are and the historian is willing and anxious to look at them each in its own right. Such an editor might now be willing to reprint one document with a historical apparatus as a fuller presentation of the whole work, but the attitude toward eclecticism will remain hostile. The sociologist, who claimed the work was whatever text the author and publisher together produced (whether in harmony or tension), may now see that the work is more than a text. Such an editor will still wish to include as an integral part of the work the publisher's contributions to it, and he will probably still want as the reading text a product of the social contract, but the work must include some aspect of its development and variation regardless of how inclusive the authoritative net becomes. The aesthetician, too, will still construct an eclectic text that satisfies the dictates of his aesthetic creed, but he cannot fail to see that his response to what he considers the best text of the work is influenced and enriched by his response to the historical forms of the work.

And so, regardless of formal orientation, an edition of a work must consist of more than a text. But a text is what all editions must begin with. There are three basic choices: (1) a text identical to that in a historical document, (2) a text representing a historically identifiable "version," as previously defined, or (3) a text that mixes material from two or more versions according to some critical dictum.

Because the first of these makes no attempt to rescue an authorial version from the available texts, the authorial editor sees it as no more than a source book for the work of art. The work of freeing authorial material from the patina of compositorial or editorial intervention is left entirely to the reader. The historian and the sociologist, who view these things differently, might be happy with such a text.

The second, because it attempts to separate authorial from nonauthorial forms found in the documentary texts and because it tries to maintain distinctions between authorial versions in the historical progression of revisions, is a critical text—some would say an eclectic text. The critical faculty of the editor is directed toward making historical, not aesthetic, distinctions as he sets out chronologically the author's development and revision of the work. The choice for a clear-reading text can be any one of the distinguishable versions, and the apparatus is likely to show the pre– and post–reading-text variants in historical progression.

The third, properly called an eclectic text, provides what the editor and many readers may consider the most satisfying initial aesthetic experience of a work, though many attempts to provide such texts in the past have provoked disagreement and some entertaining academic word wars about the criteria used in selecting readings for the clear text.[7] It is hard to conceive an apparatus for an eclectic text in which the historical progression of versions can be portrayed in an orderly fashion. For a student of the work this drawback may outweigh the modicum of increased aesthetic pleasure gained from an eclectic reading text. Yet the problem of editing and sorting out versions is a complex one. For example, authors occasionally violate the historical integrity of versions of their works by transferring blocks of text from one version to another—sometimes ignoring the fact that revisions in parts of the text render inappropriate passages in the reused blocks. When an editor identifies such failures to revise adequately during the development of a version, an editorial problem arises that can be seen more clearly from the perspective gained by my definitions. This clarity of view may reveal the problem to be more complex than the editor originally thought—but that is no reason to discard the definitions. Tracing of composition may make each version, with its flaws, more understandable to readers. Or one may even conclude that the reader needs to confront a text that is internally more coherent than one that is strictly faithful to a historical moment in the author's conception of the work. Either way, both editor and critic gain from the discovery and exposure, rather than the glossing over, of the author's failure to take care of all the details in the work.

Aesthetically conceived versions of a work may be as worthwhile as historically conceived versions or sociological or documentary versions. But editors and readers and critics should know what *version* they are look-

---

7. Notable examples are the controversies over the way to edit Stephen Crane's *Maggie* (Fredson Bowers, Hershel Parker, Donald Pizer, and Joseph Katz), Crane's *The Red Badge of Courage* (Henry Binder, Bowers, Parker, and Pizer), Theodore Dreiser's *Sister Carrie* (James West and Pizer), F. Scott Fitzgerald's *Tender Is the Night* (Malcolm Cowley, Matthew Bruccoli, and Parker), and William Faulkner's *Flags in the Dust* (Douglas Day and Thomas McHaney). Most of these arguments involve other editorial principles in addition to aesthetics.

ing at and what aspects of the *work* are obscured by the editorial choices involved.

An edited text can present only one version at a time in clear-reading form, but the authorial variants representing the other versions can accompany that text, making the work—the imagined whole implied by the differing versions—more fully accessible. Readers confront a work of art for the first time in one text: the one they read. If they stop there, they limit their acquaintance with the work of art—the imagined whole implied by its variant forms—to that which the printing medium is capable of presenting on the pages of a clear-reading printed text. Students returning to the work of art ferret out the author's intended work by contemplating the text and its variant *authorial* forms. To do this critics need access to authorial forms in historical perspective. (They need a great many other things as well, but my point here is about the text and apparatus that is the printed representation of the author's work of art.)

What no editor *can* do is compress a work into a single best version corresponding to *the* author's intention. Such a goal is usually self-contradictory. As long as the textual situation remains relatively simple, perhaps a single best text can be produced because the historical and aesthetic values are not far enough apart to entail noticeable sacrifices of the one to the other. But when facing a complicated problem—say Dreiser's *Sister Carrie* or Irving's *Conquest of Granada* or, as I try to show in part 2, Crane's *Red Badge of Courage*—the consequence of following an editorial theory of the author's final intentions or best intentions in order to establish the single most reliable text is to raise eyebrows all round, since the critical choices not only are complex but also affect undeniably the meaning of the work.

But one need not see the problem only from within the authorial orientation. Sociologists, historians, and aestheticians are usually also interested in change and development. A sociological orientation is in a way merely an extension of the authorial. The work of art is the whole implied not just by the authorial forms but, perhaps just as important, by its editorial forms. The historian may be as interested in how a document came into being as the aesthetician is, though he does not approve of changing the documentary text into some nonhistorical form of itself.[8]

My main point, again, is that editors edit because texts often fail to *do* what editors want them to do. There are differences of desire among

---

8. Actually, many historians, editors of historical papers, do considerable editing of "accidentals" for readability and consistency while refusing to mix substantives from distinct historical documents.

editors that lead them to do things in different ways—to value some aspects of text over others, to admit into the text some things but not others. But all editors are interested in processes of composition and transmission of texts. Heretofore, editors have allowed their formal orientation to dictate what the *right* text shall be for all the users of their editions. But, if we shift the emphasis from "the right text" to "the whole work," the editor can prepare the text according to his preferred orientation and provide an apparatus usable by persons with other preferences. This has been the ideal of scholarly editions for years, but a failure to appreciate the extent to which a formal orientation influences the text and the viability of other orientations has kept editors from being sufficiently careful about making apparatuses readily usable. I return to this subject in the chapter on copy-texts and apparatuses.

Chapter Five

Expectations

With the discussion of textual authority and formal orientations as a background to help us understand differences of opinion on how to proceed with an editorial problem, and with the discussion of intention and the materials of literary art to help us see the complexity and perhaps the indeterminacy of literary works of art, we can focus attention on an aspect of the editorial problem that lies at the root of Gaskell's, McGann's, Stillinger's, and Reiman's difficulties with Bowers's and Tanselle's emphasis on the authorial forms in manuscripts. Each of these editors has worked closely with enough manuscripts and traced enough publisher-author relationships to know that authors expect publishers and their minions to do certain things for them. Good publishers do the job well; bad publishers make authors climb the walls. But authors usually do not manufacture and publish their own works—so publication is a social endeavor. Furthermore, authors and publishers both tend to treat manuscripts as tentative forms of the work. Recognizing these things, McGann and others seem puzzled by Bowers's and Tanselle's insistence on the authority of manuscripts. Works that publishers have produced badly can justify a continued interest in the manuscript, they say, but ordinary practice indicates that authors not only need publishers to actualize their works, they also enter agreements to supply works that publishers (and the public) desire. In a sense, then, authors work to order, and the desires of the publisher and public are exercised in a variety of ways, including self-censorship, catering to public taste, censorship, and basic assistance in rationalizing accidentals and providing book design and distribution of the resulting socialized commodity.

Greg's rationale for choice of copy-text, we recall, depends on a division of authority for substantives and accidentals, and this division depends on an analysis of "usual practice" in the production of books. We should also recall that the only reason to choose a copy-text and to follow its readings when in doubt about which is the authoritative reading (or the preferred reading or the authorial reading) is that editors are frequently confronted with situations in which the evidence is missing or ambiguous. If there were no doubt about these matters, one would simply do what was "undoubtedly" the right thing. But, in the absence of conclusive evidence, choosing a copy-text and relying primarily on its readings is an expedient deemed necessary and useful. Finally, we should recall that a rationale for choice of copy-text is different from a rationale for emendation.

Greg's idea was that usually authors, when inscribing manuscripts and correcting proofs, focus primarily on the words and word order rather than on spelling, punctuation, capitalization, or italics—matters they normally leave to the publisher's crew to rationalize. Greg and everyone else knows that sometimes authors pay meticulous attention to accidentals: we have the examples of A. E. Housman and Max Beerbohm, and we have conflicting reports about Mark Twain and John Dryden, to mention a few.[1] But in all such cases evidence survives to prove that the authors desired to exercise control; however, instances in which authors relied on the publisher or simply did not fight the production crew's control over accidentals are, it seems, more numerous.

It seems clear to me that an editor's fundamental orientation, not the intrinsic merits of any textual problem, determines the assessment of the problem and the solution provided. The execution of those solutions depends, furthermore, on the competence of the editor to fulfill the demands of the system chosen. If the author is the final authority but either delegates or *allows* the text to be manipulated by others, an editor will wish to eliminate that manipulation or adjudicate it according to the sense of authority and delegation of it that the editor brings to the case. If a social interdependence between author and book producers authorizes the text, an editor will tend to respect the manipulation of the author's work and will intervene, if at all, only when that socializing process appears to have violated (perhaps through error, incompetence, or accident) its own principles.

The test of these principles does not come in situations in which all the evidence survives or in which the delegation of authority is detailed and

---

1. See James Thorpe's *Watching the P&Qs: Editorial Treatment of Accidentals*, University of Kansas Library Series 38 (University of Kansas Libraries, 1971); reprinted in *Principles of Textual Criticism* (San Marino: Huntington Library, 1972).

explicit. It comes in cases of high ambiguity. To clarify the issues involved I would like to examine the problems arising from an author who gives an imperfect manuscript to the printer, who supplies needed but nonauthorial polishing. This may not be as exciting a problem as that presented by the ten drafts and two final versions of Fitzgerald's *Tender Is the Night*[2] or the two versions of the manuscript and ten or so published versions of Hardy's *Tess of the D'Urbervilles*,[3] but, by focusing on what is often considered trivial, I hope to demonstrate not only the intricacies of the editorial problem but also the importance of the details.

It will not escape notice that the controversy detailed here lies primarily within the authorial orientation, but, before editors who have already rejected that orientation abandon this chapter, I should emphasize my belief that the details of this controversy show what is at stake in abandoning the pursuit of authorial intentions. Put simply, we have, in artifacts, what the author did (if we have manuscripts and proof corrections), what the publisher did (in the first edition), and what other publishers did (in other editions). Any editorial procedure that selects one extant version over others or that arrays extant texts in relation to one another, essentially reprints and focuses attention on an already accomplished text.[4] The following problem, in a trivial way, shows that an edition that pursues the intentions of one originator (say the author), produces a text that did not exist before and, therefore, adds to the array of texts already available. From the authorial point of view this addition is valuable as a process of historical restoration or purification of texts; from the sociological point of view this addition is a corruption, a mixed breed, an unnecessary violation of both history and its social conditions.

Tanselle describes the general problem as "determining what relation authorial expectation bears to intention."[5] This is to state the problem

2. Matthew Bruccoli, *The Composition of* Tender Is the Night (Pittsburgh: University of Pittsburgh Press, 1963).

3. John Laird, "New Light on the Evolution of *Tess of the D'Urbervilles*," *Review of English Studies* 31 (Nov. 1980): 414–15.

4. There is a growing body of commentary endorsing the historicizing and tracing of the development of existing texts as the primary objects of textual criticism in place of earlier traditions of emending or correcting texts to produce new and better ones. See Morris Eaves, "'Why Don't They Leave It Alone?' Speculations on the Authority of Audience in Editorial Theory," in *Cultural Artifacts and the Production of Meaning: The Page, the Image, and the Body*, ed. Margaret J. M. Ezell and Katherine O'Brien O'Keeffe (Ann Arbor: University of Michigan Press, 1994), 85–99.

5. Tanselle, "Recent Editorial Discussion and the Central Questions of Editing," *Studies in Bibliography* 34 (1981): 62–63.

from within the authorial orientation, the only place in which it is a problem, since the historian sees a manuscript text and a printed text—each distinct—and a sociological editor wonders what the fuss is all about. It is important, nevertheless, to distinguish between "intention" and "expectation," because a concept of expectation lies at the root of some arguments for the sociological orientation.[6] Tanselle reflects the authorial bias when he says that "readers of scholarly critical editions are primarily interested in what the author did rather than what a publisher's editor did," but that does not limit the importance of his suggestion that, just because an "author expected certain alterations to be carried out in the publisher's office," it does not follow that we should accept everything that was done there as a fulfillment of his expectations.[7]

From Tanselle's and McGann's opposing viewpoints it would appear that the editor is faced with choosing to represent what the author did (the manuscript) or what the publisher did (the printed work). But in many cases the former is not what the author *wished* to see in print, and the latter is not what the author *did*—and perhaps it is not what he wished, either. For, in fact, it often happens that what the author *did* was to leave certain things for the publisher to do for him and what the publisher *did* was to do that and more besides. The editor has a third choice: to edit a text that does for the author what he expected to have done for him but avoids the extraneous alterations imposed by a publisher in his normal but misguided undertaking of the production process. The result, as I have said elsewhere, "will be much closer to 'what the author did' than blanket acceptance of copy-text forms."[8] It should be remembered, too, however, that the result of any emendation is a critical text.

To illustrate these generalizations let us turn to the specific editorial problems posed by W. M. Thackeray's manuscripts for his novels. Editorial problems all have contexts that influence how we assess the specific evidence, and so it is necessary to present the context. In order to introduce the problem of Thackeray's alleged expectations for punctuation, I need to make four points. The first is to indicate how experienced a writer

---

6. For example, arguments for the sociological orientation proceeding from an unacknowledged allegiance to the authorial orientation suggest that the social contract is entered into willingly by authors "seeking help" with the production of "their work" or suggest that production processes fulfill the intention of the author to be published in a conventional way. Truly sociological arguments acknowledge that there is an opposition between the social and authorial (individual) orientations and that fulfillment of one entails rejection of the other.

7. Tanselle, "Recent Editorial Discussion," 62–63.

8. Peter L. Shillingsburg, "Key Issues in Editorial Theory," *Analytical & Enumerative Bibliography* 6 (1982): 13.

he was. The second is to explore the relationship between Thackeray and the compositors who altered his punctuation. The third is to explain the principles by which compositors adopted responsibility for the punctuation. The fourth is to delineate in general terms the alternative systems for punctuation in current practice when Thackeray wrote and compositors typeset his books.

When, in 1846, Thackeray came to Bradbury and Evans with the first five chapters of *Vanity Fair*, he had had at least ten years of hand-to-mouth experience in journalism. He was a professional writer. He had contributed regularly to two periodicals of which he was part owner and to several periodicals of international standing, such as *Fraser's* and the *New Monthly*. And he was the author of five books published by contract. In short, he knew the business of writing, the business of editing, and the business of book and periodical production. Furthermore, having worked since 1842 for *Punch,* he was familiar with Bradbury and Evans's compositors. From 1847 through 1859 most of his writing was set in type by the Bradbury and Evans compositors, for, even though *Henry Esmond* was published by Smith, Elder and Company, it was typeset and printed by Bradbury and Evans. Some of the compositors' names that appear on the manuscript of *Vanity Fair* reappear on the manuscripts of *Pendennis, Esmond,* and *The Newcomes.* We should bear in mind, then, that Thackeray's manuscripts were written by a man who knew what compositors did.

I do not know whether Thackeray left routine punctuation to the compositor because he did not care what they did to it or because he knew full well that they would impose their own system of punctuation regardless of what he did. We know compositors routinely imposed their own, or their shop's, punctuation systems, because comparisons of manuscripts with first editions of mid-nineteenth-century books usually reveal extensive alterations in punctuation. Examples abound. George Washington Irving's manuscripts (there were two) for *The Conquest of Granada* are adequately punctuated even by modern standards, but both the English and the U.S. publishers added considerable amounts of conventional though unnecessary punctuation. Charlotte Brontë wrote to Smith, Elder and Company thanking them for what the compositors had done to her punctuation in *Jane Eyre,* though at least one modern critic declared the manuscript punctuation adequate and the editors of the Clarendon edition, which adopted the punctuation of the first edition because of Brontë's gratitude, never said the manuscript was inadequate. Mark Twain claimed to have cabled his publisher to have a compositor shot without time to pray for what he had done to Twain's punctuation. Harper and Brothers had an elaborate system for punctuation and spelling, which they imposed on Thackeray's U.S. reprints—both when they were "pirating" (it was not illegal) his works and later, when they became his authorized publishers—while, on the other hand, Appleton and Company, also of New York, were much more flexible or much less meddlesome, leaving Thackeray's punctuation and spelling relatively untouched.[9]

It was from the attempt to figure out what system was being imposed on Thackeray's prose by his various publishers, and from the attempt to reconcile what they had done with what contemporary printers' manuals advocated, that I stumbled upon what I should have made it my business from the beginning to know: that the principles for punctuation taught in schools and imposed by printers were in a state of flux in the middle of the nineteenth century (as, indeed, they still are). What Thackeray had been taught in school was a system of punctuation based primarily on concepts of rhetoric and elocution, rather than primarily on grammar and syntax. The rhetorical system was still the basis for advice and training in printers' manuals as late as 1838, but printers in the trade were rapidly replacing it in practice with syntactical punctuation, as an examination of any of the books and periodicals published by Bradbury and Evans in the 1840s will reveal.

The basic concept of rhetorical punctuation is that different points indicate different lengths of pauses. Thus, a comma is a short pause, a semicolon indicates a pause twice as long as that for a comma, a colon represents a pause three times as long as that for a comma, and a pause following a period is four times as long as that for a comma. (This information I have taken from C. H. Timperley's *The Printers' Manual*, published by H. Johnson in London in 1838, a book that also laments the ignorance of most writers in the art of punctuation and fantasizes about a world in which authors turn in manuscripts with no punctuation at all, leaving that chore to the professional competence of the compositors.)

So, we turn to Thackeray's manuscripts, remembering that they are the product of a knowledgeable, professional writer, writing for the eyes of compositors who were familiar with his manuscripts and with whose work he was familiar. We are looking at the writing of a man who punc-

---

9. These observations are based on complete collations of the English source texts with the U.S. reprints of *Pendennis, Vanity Fair, Esmond, The Yellowplush Papers, The Newcomes,* and *Mr. Brown's Letters to a Young Man about Town*.

tuated rhetorically but who was accustomed to compositors who imposed syntactical punctuation on his texts.[10]

On first examination the manuscripts appear "raw" or at best uneven. Quotation marks, when present, are usually single quotes; they are seldom paired, more frequently opened than closed. Often quotations are opened by a dash and closed by a comma, a *said so-and-so* or not at all. Commas, which we expect to attend quotations, are more often missing than present. Nouns of address are seldom set off by commas, and paragraphs often end with no punctuation at all. Apostrophes, whether to show possession or contraction, are seldom present. Abbreviations are inconsistently followed by periods, and sentences ending in question marks or exclamation points often also have an extraneous period. Appositives are more often than not set off by commas, but no discernible pattern exists. Words or elements in series usually lack commas. These characteristics have led all previous commentators to call Thackeray a careless writer.

But there the catalog of deficiencies stops. Aside from these highly routine matters, which affect the polish but not the meaning of the text, the manuscripts are adequately and sometimes very expressively punctuated. The following examples are quoted, with permission, from Edgar Harden's textual introduction to his edition of *Esmond*.[11]

> An example from ... [vol. 2] shows a compositor (Turner) evidently failing to understand Thackeray's delicate use of semicolon and colon, and instead, obliterating them by imposing regularizing commas, thereby making the sentence read: "Esmond took his handkerchief when his nurse left him, and very likely kissed it, and looked at the bauble embroidered in the corner" (II, 12.23–5). . . . Anyone with a commitment to Thackeray's active intentions, however, and a responsiveness to the subtle discriminations of his style, could be expected to recognize that Thackeray's manuscript embodies not only an active authorial intention, but a literary purpose and meaning whose precision and nuance have been blunted. Thackeray poises the sentence over a dividing semicolon that distinguishes between what Esmond actually did and what he "very likely" did; Thackeray then links the last

---

10. For a detailed analysis of this issue as it relates to Thomas Hardy's works, see the last chapter of Simon Gatrell's *Hardy the Creator* (Charlottesville: University Press of Virginia, 1993). It concludes ringingly in favor of Hardy's eccentric punctuation over the compositors' professional homogenization.

11. Edgar Harden, intro. to W. M. Thackeray, *Esmond* (New York: Garland, 1989), 419–20.

two clauses with a colon. He also makes the reader pause over these two punctuation marks for ever so slightly longer and more emotionally expressive a mini-second than a reader would pause over commas. For these reasons, this edition follows the manuscript in reading: "Esmond took his handkerchief when his nurse left him; and very likely kissed it: and looked at the bauble embroidered in the corner."

More complex as well as more serious examples of punctuational intervention can be illustrated by the following sentence, which reads in [the first edition] as follows: "But, as a prodigal that's sending in a schedule of his debts to his friends, never puts all down, and, you may be sure, the rogue keeps back some immense swingeing bill, that he doesn't dare to own; so the poor Frank had a very heavy piece of news to break to his mother, and which he hadn't the courage to introduce into his first confession" (III, 46.17–24). In one instance, compositorial change seems appropriate, but otherwise this sentence has been clotted and its rhythm abundantly thwarted. The latter effect, which occurs frequently in the [printed] text, can be identified as the result of compositorial habit. Thackeray wrote: "But,—as a prodigal that's sending in a schedule of his debts to his friends never puts all down, and you may be sure the rogue keeps back some immense swinging bill that he doesn't dare at first to own—so my poor Frank had a very heavy piece of news to break to his mother, and wh. he hadn't the courage to introduce into his first confession." In proof stage, Thackeray was evidently concerned with deleting "at first" and changing "swinging" to "swingeing." He [apparently] did not notice that the compositor had misread "my" as "the" (partly understandable, given the handwriting), and he passively accepted Sweeting's punctuation.

Besides breaking Thackeray's fluid prose into small syntactical units, the compositor typically resisted Thackeray's use of dashes. Hence the 1852 [edition] began: "But, as a prodigal ...." This alteration was minor, though unnecessary, but all other punctuational changes seem to stifle Thackeray's active purpose embodied in the manuscript sentence. Therefore this edition prints the following version: "But,—as a prodigal that's sending in a schedule of his debts to his friends never puts all down, and you may be sure the rogue keeps back some immense swingeing bill that he doesn't dare to own—so my poor Frank had a very heavy piece of news to break to his mother, and which he hadn't the courage to introduce into his first confession." The sentence is a typically long Thackerayan period, but one to which he gave utter clarity of structure and compellingness of rhythm, as its two-part subordination leads to the central pause marked by the dash preceding "so," which is then followed by the sentence's two-part conclusion. One of the most notable effects of this edition's decision to follow the author's active intentions as they are embodied in the manuscript copy-text, therefore, will be to make the rhythms of his prose much more accessible to the reader than they have hitherto been.

Harden makes a good first step toward convincing us that Thackeray's choice of punctuation is not only viable but superior in many respects to that imposed on him by his compositors.[12] But Harden's remark about Thackeray passively accepting Sweeting's punctuation is worth pausing over, for it echoes arguments that have been used for years to support the choice of printed texts over manuscripts as copy-texts when the author fails to express disapproval of compositorial forms—or when the evidence that the author disapproved has failed to survive. The fact is, we do not know whether Thackeray approved Sweeting's punctuation or simply failed to note it. He may, for all the evidence adducible, have bitten his lip and decided not to leave a written record of his bitter disappointment at Sweeting's punctuation. Editorial appeals to an author's tacit approval or passive acceptance remind me of Porphyria's lover in Browning's poem who cradled the head of his beloved victim all night while God tacitly approved his crime.

Although the examples given thus far do not show it very well, the manuscript does not represent "finished" copy. This is so not because it needs pruning by an editor like Maxwell Perkins but because the conventions of punctuation for published books have not been observed. What I am trying to demonstrate is that Thackeray's manuscripts needed work—whether he intended them to be reworked or just expected that they would be, or even if he never noticed or cared. There are many conventions for punctuation, and, insofar as Thackeray followed an established convention in punctuation, it tended to be rhetorical. (People who have never heard

---

12. One could argue that superiority can be established only by aesthetic standards; therefore, the historical fact of the compositor's work might be a more compelling editorial goal than the aesthetic tastes of the modern editors trying to rehabilitate the author as an artistic construct. But, by the standard of added value, we already have the work of the compositors in the first edition, reproducible by photographic means; whereas, before Harden's edition, we had no copy of the work that fulfills what appear to be Thackeray's intentions or expectations.

of the rules for rhetorical punctuation but who recognize that apparently unorthodox pointing seems to work often say that it is "punctuation by ear.") But Thackeray turned his manuscript over to printers who provided a finishing system that observes a different convention. His publishers did not recognize or did not try to fulfill the potential of Thackeray's rhetorical system. They substituted a different, a syntactical, one. Both the rhetorical and syntactic systems are internally coherent. Applied to the same passage of prose, both systems would mark many points in exactly the same way. But syntactical punctuation is much more regular or predictable than rhetorical punctuation, which is individualistic and often eccentric. Syntactical punctuation's regularity and susceptibility to rules is probably why it has become the convention of preference with printers and schoolteachers. Rhetorical punctuation is individualistic and shows nuances of expression far more subtly than syntactical punctuation.

Let us pause a moment before a Thackeray manuscript and see what our editorial orientations toward forms will incline us to do. First, we will remember that we are editing his work because we think Thackeray is a great writer, because we want to know what he wrote and how he wrote it—or, to put it in less adoringly authorial terms, we want to see what the text says and how it says it. A documentary orientation will say the manuscript is authorial, incomplete, and poorly presented in many of its formal details. It will not do as a published work, but it has historical interest and integrity. The first edition, the documentary historian continues, is complete and adequately conventional for publication but in certain serious ways alters the text to reflect mid-nineteenth-century printing house practice. It, too, has its interest and historical integrity. The sociological orientation would pick up on this note, reiterating its belief that publishers and editors (or in this case compositors) are a necessary fact of the world of literary art and that we should be grateful for the "actualizing" work that transformed the unfinished manuscript into a book. The altered punctuation was a part of the job of bringing to the modern reading public the work of a man carelessly using a system rapidly falling into disuse. As for the author's punctuation, if indeed it followed a recognizable system, it failed to do so with the consistency required for a published book. The social contract that Thackeray as a professional writer entered into with his publisher allowed him to insist on his own forms if he wished. His failure to do so indicates that he expected or at least accepted the publisher's work as a fulfillment of the publishing contract.

An editor with an authorial orientation winces at this argument, for, though he must agree that the manuscript is unfinished and needs work, he is unhappy with this embrace of nonauthorial forms. What brought him to the task was a love for *Thackeray's* art. What he has found out about the text by comparing manuscript and first edition is that an expressive and subtle part of Thackeray's art got short shrift from both the author and the publisher. In fact, for that part of the work the published version substitutes the compositor's professional rectitude for the author's natural expression. And so the authorial editor digs in his heels and, in the words of the sociologist, actualizes the manuscript text himself, providing what the unfinished manuscript needs but respecting the system that is already there in the manuscript—as if the social contract existed between the author and himself.

Historical, sociological, and aesthetic editors will all frown on these efforts, each for different reasons. But, if the first edition does not represent what the author *did* and the manuscript does not represent what he *intended*, what is the editor with an authorial orientation to do? Intention, a thing of the mind and of the past, is by nature irrecoverable. The editor who is to pursue Thackeray's intentions or fulfill his expectations, must do so not by accepting one unsatisfactory text (the first edition) over another unsatisfactory text (the manuscript) but, rather, by exercising critical judgment in choices aimed at approximating the irrecoverable. The best one can hope for is a *less* unsatisfactory text. For me, that is better than a *patently* unsatisfactory text as represented in either the manuscript or the first edition. Experience has shown me, however, that the results are unappreciated by those who hold other formal orientations or who believe in an author's tacit approval of first-edition forms.

Actually, in the case of *Vanity Fair* there are two arguments for selecting the first edition for copy-text. One is that the published version represents the fulfillment of the publishing contract Thackeray willingly entered into and is the text he proofread and approved. The other is that only a partial manuscript survives (about one-sixth of the novel), so that choosing the manuscript for copy-text forces a dual character on the accidentals of the book, since what can be done to the punctuation in the parts for which manuscript survives cannot be done for the rest of the book. An editor must weigh losses and gains involved in either approach. Is it more important to have a relatively consistent, though nonauthorial, texture of punctuation throughout the novel or to have the author's punctuation instead of the compositor's when it is possible to do so? My choice was to have as much of Thackeray's writing style as possible, warning my readers of the overlay of compositorial forms affecting chapters 7 and 14 through 67, for which no manuscript survives.

Even when two editors agree in principle that the rhetorical punctuation of a manuscript must be retained while routine conventional matters must be emended, resulting in a new text different from both the manuscript and the first edition, these editors may not agree about which specific emendations are desirable. (See, for example, the additional examples in the table of parallel texts that follows. Notice particularly in the examples from *The Newcomes* that the difference between Thackeray's and the compositors' systems is not merely a difference between "light" and "heavy" pointing.)

I do not expect agreement about how these passages should be punctuated. My point is that, even with the guidance of Greg's rationale for copy-text, the treatment of punctuation is a complex issue within the authorial orientation. Furthermore, adopting a sociological or historical orientation does not simplify matters, though they both impose simple solutions, because readers and critics may still legitimately be interested in a textual style or texture that is obscured by the blanket adoption of either manuscript or first-edition forms. Different rationales for choice of copy-text and for emendation make differences in the texts that can be discerned critically. Hence, editors must not take lightly the different requirements that scholars bring to edited texts.

I suppose the big questions in *Vanity Fair* are: was Becky or was she not unfaithful to Crawley with Lord Steyne? And did she or did she not poison Jos for his life insurance? And, if the answers to these questions cast a shadow on that lady's character, Thackeray asks a more important question—one not typical of his age: who among you is there without sin who can cast the first stone? In light of these kinds of questions one wonders whether to spend much time or effort on Thackeray's punctuation. But an examination of the problem does illustrate the difficulties of satisfying the critic's desire to get at the text Thackeray wrote—or wanted to write or should have written—while adhering closely to traditionally held editorial principles. It also illustrates how differing orientations influence the editor toward different concepts of what is textually significant and what is not.

It is easy to see that the manuscript reading of the passage in *Esmond* in which Rachel leads her ward "hat in hand" to his bedroom on his return from college is a reading far more consistent with the progression of events and character development than the first-edition *mis*reading in which Rachel and her tall ward go "hand in hand" to the bedroom. Is it just as important to see Thackeray's prose as he wrote it, following an archaic, highly individualistic system of punctuation, with an inconsistent combination of delicate precision and gross inattention? Would Thackeray studies be better off sticking to the larger questions? Are readers better served by the first-edition forms reflecting compositorial competence in routine and syntactical punctuation or by a raw transcript of the manuscript? Whatever the case, if literary critics tune in to the evidence of rhetoric provided by punctuation, they will be rewarded in doing so only if they use texts that have not been *copyedited* either by commercial compositors or by scholarly editors.

Whether or not Thackeray's punctuation raises questions of importance to literary critics, it does shed light on the reasons we pursue an author's intentions and on the rationale for the choice of copy-text. First, critics interested in reading Thackeray as stylist or prosodist cannot rely on just any old text. Such students certainly cannot rely on the first edition. And, if they try to rely on the manuscripts, they must distinguish between those marks that are meaningfully present or absent and those that are carelessly dashed in or left out. Second, compositors were not fully aware of what was going on in the text because their understanding of their own job did not require it. They did not have time to figure out the rhetorical effect of Thackeray's punctuation. And so, if *we* prefer to deal with the author—who may have been eccentric and may even have been careless about some conventional punctuation but who did have a system of punctuation and, even more important, who did know what was going on—we must find an edition, or make one, that reflects authorial forms, both intention and expectation. Third, we see that Greg's rationale for the choice of copy-text (designed to recover as much as possible of the author's accidentals) assumes that authorial forms are potentially more interesting than compositorial forms.[13]

Authorial expectations can be thought of as unrecorded intentions to do something. Not only did Thackeray never go on record with his opinion of or standards for punctuation, but we have only two corrupt sources for a record of his intention for the printed work: the manuscript, deficient because of its use of a shorthand elision of punctuation, and the first edition,

---

13. McGann holds that Greg sought to preserve authorial accidentals not because he wished to recover the author's intentions but because the accidentals were more chaotic in subsequent printed texts of the works that Greg was interested in. He implies that, had the printed texts had a more consistent texture of accidentals, Greg would not have preferred the author's forms (McGann, *Critique of Modern Textual Criticism* [Chicago: University of Chicago Press, 1983], 28–30). It is an interesting argument, which I find unconvincing. Consistency, if it is valued, can easily be imposed on a text without reference to an authoritative source.

drastically altered by compositorial intervention. The editor who wants the text to be what Thackeray intended it to be must be prepared to have every other critic disagree with his choices. Even if he does nothing, he cannot please everyone. Whatever it is, the rationale for emendation of the chosen copy-text must identify and defend the text and the particular orientation toward its formal elements that *is to be* the editorial goal and distinguish that text from among the several authorial or socially or historically interesting texts that *might have been* the editorial goal. There is seldom if ever a single *right* editorial goal.

What I hope this extended example from *Vanity Fair* has demonstrated is that the problem of expectations is real and important to editors of both authorial and sociological orientations. Beyond that I hope it has shown that a close look at what happens in the production process, an actual look into the workshop in which McGann places the author-publisher relationship, will help the editor assess the fulfillment of authorial expectations by the contract he enters into with the publisher. Tanselle, as I said before, observes that an author's reliance on a publisher for some alterations need not commit us, as editors, to accept all that the publisher does. Choosing what to do about authorial expectations must be based not on a theory about socialization of texts but, instead, on the actual evidence about how, in every detail, the publisher went about fulfilling the expectations.

TABLE OF PARALLEL TEXTS

The following passages are intended to demonstrate what the compositors of the first editions of several of Thackeray's works did with his punctuation and how an editor might treat the manuscript differently in an attempt to preserve the rhetorical system that operates in the manuscripts. The examples from *Esmond* show how two editors who agree in principle nevertheless edit differently.

Example 1, from *Esmond*

> *First Edition:* I have seen in his very old age and decrepitude the old French King Lewis the Fourteenth, the type and model of king-hood—who never moved but to measure, who lived and died according to the laws of his Court-Marshal, persisting in enacting through life the part of Hero; and divested of poetry, this was but a little wrinkled old man, pock-marked, and with a great periwig and red heels

to make him look tall,—a hero for a book if you like, or for a brass statue or a painted-ceiling, a god in a Roman shape, but what more than a man for Madame Maintenon, or the barber who shaved him, or Monsieur Fagon his surgeon?

Manuscript: I have seen in his very old age and decrepitude the old French King Lewis XIV—the type and model of King-dom, who never moved but to measure, who lived and died according to the laws of his Court-Marshal, persisting in enacting through life the part of Hero; and divested of Poetry, this was but a little wrinkled old man, pock-marked and with a great perriwig and red heels to make him look tall,—a hero for a book if you like or for a brass statue or a painted ciel-ing a God in a Roman Shape, but what more than a man for Madame Maintenon, or the barber who shaved him, or Monsieur Fagon his Surgeon?

Editor A emendations in the Manuscript: *line 2:* King-hood, / *line 8:* cieling,

Editor B emendations in the Manuscript: *line 2:* the Fourteenth —the / *line 2:* King-hood, / *line 8:* cieling, / *line 8:* god / *line 8:* shape,

Example 2, from *Esmond*

First Edition: This resolute old loyalist who was with the King whilst his house was thus being battered down, escaped abroad with his only son then a boy, to return and take a part in Worcester fight. On that fatal field Eustace Esmond was killed, and Castlewood fled from it once more into exile, and henceforward, and after the Restoration, never was away from the Court of the monarch (for whose return we offer thanks in the Prayer Book) who sold his country and who took bribes of the French king.

Manuscript: This resolute old loyalist was with the King whilst his house was thus being battered down: escaped abroad with his only Son then a boy, to return and take a part in Worcester fight. On that fa-tal field Eustace Esmond was killed, and Castlewood fled from it once more into exile, and henceforward and after the Restoration never was away from the Court of the Monarch who sold his Country, and for whose return we offer thank in the Prayer-book, and who took bribes of the French King.

Editor A emendations in the Manuscript: *lines 6–8:* Monarch (for whose return we offer thanks in the Prayer-book) who sold his country and who took bribes of the French King.

Editor B emendations in the Manuscript: *line 1:* loyalist, who was / *line 2:* down, / *line 3:* Son, / *lines 6–8:* monarch (for whose return we offer thanks in the Prayer-book) who sold his country and who took bribes of the French King.

Example 3, from *Esmond*

First Edition: Starve me, keep me from books and honest people, educate me to love dice, and gin, and pleasure, and put me on Hounslow Heath, with a purse before me and I will take it.

Manuscript: Starve me: keep me from books & honest people educate me to love dice gin & pleasure and put me on Hounslow Heath with a purse before me & I will take it.

Editor A emendations in the Manuscript: *lines 1–3:* [expand ampersands to *and*] / *line 1:* people,

Editor B emendations in the Manuscript: *lines 1–3:* [expand ampersands to *and*] / *line 1:* people, / *lines 2:* dice, / *line 2:* gin, and pleasure,

The basic difference between the texts produced by editors A and B (real editors whose names are suppressed to protect both innocent and guilty) is the degree to which pauses inspired by the syntax alone seem requisite for editor B but extraneous to editor A. In no instance is the difference one affecting meaning.

There follow some examples from other works with emendations by editor A only.

Example 4, from *The Newcomes*

First Edition: On the same evening—as he was biting his nails, or cursing his fate, or wishing to invite Lord Faringtosh into the neighbouring garden of Berkeley Square, whence the policeman might carry to the station-house the corpse of the survivor, Lady Kew would bow to him with perfect graciousness; on other nights her ladyship would pass . . . .

Manuscript: On the same evening as he was biting his nails or cursing his fate or wishing to invite Lord Faringtosh into the neighbouring garden of Berkeley Square; whence the policeman might carry to the station-house the corpse of the survivor—Lady Kew would bow to him with perfect graciousness, smile and ask him how his studies were going on, and if he had heard from his father and regret that she was not at home when he called once. On other nights her ladyship would pass . . . .

Editor A emendations in the Manuscript: *None*

Example 5, from *The Newcomes*

First Edition: The wicked are wicked no doubt, and they go astray and they fall, and they come by their deserts: but who can measure the mischief which the very virtuous do?

Manuscript: The wicked are wicked no doubt; and they go astray, and they fall, and they come by their deserts: but who can measure the mischief wh. the very virtuous do?

Editor A emendations in the Manuscript: *line 3:* which

Example 6, from *Vanity Fair*

First Edition: Honest Jemima had all the bills, and the washing, and the mending, and the puddings, and the plate and the crockery, and the servants to superintend. But why speak about her?

Manuscript: Honest Jemima had all the bills and the washing and the mending and the puddings and the plate and crockery and the servants to superintend—but why speak of it?

Editor A emendations in the Manuscript: *None*

Example 7, from *Vanity Fair*

First Edition: In geography there is still much to be desired; and a careful and undeviating use of the backboard, for four hours daily during the next three years, is recommended

Manuscript: In geography there is still much to be desired: and a careful and undeviating use of the backboard for four hours daily during the next three years is recommended

Editor A emendations in the Manuscript: *None*

Example 8, from *Vanity Fair*

First Edition: She was small and slight in person; pale, sandy-haired, and with eyes habitually cast down: when they looked up they were very large, odd, and attractive; so attractive, that the Reverend Mr. Crisp, fresh from Oxford, and curate to the Vicar of Chiswick, the Reverend Mr. Flowerdew, fell in love with Miss Sharp; being shot dead by a glance of her eyes which was fired all the way across Chiswick Church from the school-pew to the reading-desk.

Manuscript: She was small and slight in person: pale, sandy-haired and with eyes habitually cast down; when they looked up they were very large, odd, and attractive: so attractive that the Reverend Mr. Crisp fresh from Oxford, and curate to the Vicar of Chiswick the Reverend Mr. Flowerdew fell in love with Miss Sharp, being shot dead by a glance of her eyes wh. was fired all the way across Chiswick Church from the school pew to the Reading desk.

Editor A emendations in the Manuscript: *line 5:* Flowerdew, / *line 6:* which / *line 7:* reading desk.

The rationale for this type of emendation process is certainly *not* to impose consistency or to modernize. It is to preserve as much of the author's actual practice as is compatible with a recognizable punctuation system—a basically rhetorical rather than syntactical one. Editor A believes that, in spite of its obvious inconsistencies, the system is an intelligible one, and it is Thackeray's. Further, he thinks it is superior to a more regular, syntactical system for representing the cadence of Thackeray's expression. This assessment, however, is merely critical.

Chapter Six

Completion

The foregoing exploration of the concept of authorial expectations will not make editors agree about which text should be the reading text for a scholarly edition. Editors still hold, more or less, to their various formal orientations, they still locate the authority for the work in different places, and they hold different opinions about when a work is done—finished, completed. Of course, this last concept is really the one of authority and form all over again in a new guise.

The documentary orientation, which is perhaps the most purely historical one, says the work is finished when it is written down, finished again when revised, again when printed, and again when printed again. These are points in the creative process when the text reaches stasis in a document; an editor with a documentary orientation will usually argue that the text is "finished" when it reaches a point of documentary stasis. Each documentary form is a complete record of the work at some stage in its development. The work of art is finished when it becomes a material artifact.

The bibliographic orientation concurs, adding that this is so not because of the integrity of historical moments but, rather, because of the sociomaterial significance of textuality. The logic of this position prevents, I believe, editing in any traditional sense but emphasizes an aspect of texts that has often been ignored by editors who decant the work into new wineskins, so to speak.

The sociological orientation says the work is finished when it is ready to be distributed or when intentions and expectations have been satisfactorily fulfilled in a published book and finished again when a revised edition has been published. These are references to the completion of the social processes of creating works of art that involve not just authors but book production crews. Unlike the documentary editor, for whom the integrity of the work inheres in the stability of the material text, and unlike the bibliographic editor, for whom it inheres in the sociomaterial contextualized significations, the integrity of the published book for the sociological editor derives from the group authority of its socialization, marked by publication—and marked differently by each new publication.

The aesthetic orientation probably says works of art are never really complete, that we read a work not only for what it says but also for its potential. An aesthetic approach may call for a never-ending stream of improvements or fulfillments of the potential of a work. Scholarly editors with aesthetic orientations may limit the range of improvements to those available already in the "authorial" or "authorized" documents, but independent correction of error may never end.

The authorial orientation—the one encompassing the greatest amount of internal division—says the work is finished when the author says it is, when he stops working on it, when it leaves his hand, or when it includes his "final" wishes. The notion that the work is by the author and should reflect his wishes or intentionality has dominated scholarly editing, but it is not the only possible orientation. Nor is it a unified concept, as can be illustrated from the arguments over how a single work should be edited. For example, Donald Pizer thinks that Dreiser's *Sister Carrie* should be edited to present the text Dreiser wanted after he had been influenced by his friend Arthur Henry; his publishers, Doubleday, Page, and Company; and other factors.[1] That is why he is disappointed, indignant even, with the edition of *Sister Carrie* prepared by James L. W. West III and others and published by the University of Pennsylvania Press, in which the text is based on the manuscript and short-circuits the external influences that so thoroughly affected the originally published text. (It is interesting to see Pizer begin his attack on the grounds that the new edition violates "final" authorial intention, then argue that the 1900 published text is superior critically to the original version except in its errors, and conclude with the idea that there is no "historical validity" to the original version—thus shifting his ground from one formal orientation to another as he tries to discredit a text that fails to provide what he needs for his purposes. The controversy might never have arisen had not the Pennsylvania edition appeared to offer what Pizer calls

---

1. Review of Pennsylvania *Sister Carrie, American Literature* 53 (Jan. 1982): 731–37.

a "replacement" text and had Pizer been able to see it merely as an alternative text.) West does not necessarily think his text is a better work of
art than the one Pizer wants. He sees it as a different text, an alternative form of the work, and an authorial—not a social—form.[2] Hershel
Parker has defended West's text from a slightly different perspective, reflecting his view of the creative process as having an integrity deriving from
an author's intense involvement with a work. Later revisions, Parker argues, though usually conducted with the best intentions to improve, often
have detrimental results. Parker's view is, basically, that earlier forms of
a work sometimes have a more authoritative and, critically, a better text
than some later revised versions, in which the author is acting in the role
of editor.[3]

The question central to the disagreement about how to edit *Sister Carrie* is: when was *Sister Carrie* finished? When Dreiser finished the manuscript? When his friend finished influencing the text? When the commercially prepared typescript was revised? Or when Doubleday, Page, and
Company set it in type in 1900? That is also the question basic to the
disagreements over which *The Prelude* is Wordsworth's *real* work. These
questions will be answered variously according to the formal orientation
of the answerer.

I think it is important for editors, as well as critics, to accept the legitimate existence of this variety of approaches. No single approach is the
right approach. Critics and scholars need texts for different purposes. Their
dissatisfaction with available texts is not always based on the carelessness
with which texts are commercially produced. Sometimes it is based on
the fact that a carefully produced text follows principles that thwart their
legitimate interests. Critics with historical and sociological orientations
do not want to read Bowers's eclectic text of Crane's *Maggie* (they are
not interested in Bowers, and his text confuses the things that they *are*
interested in). Students of composition and the history of development of
thought are disappointed with the Indiana C. S. Peirce edition, the Twayne
Washington Irving edition, the Indiana edition of Howells's letters, the
Princeton Thoreau edition, the SUNY Cooper edition (all of which bear
the MLA's emblem of approval from the Committee on Scholarly Editions)
because the records of manuscript alterations representing the fluctuation

---

2. James L. W. West, "Editorial Principles," in Theodore Dreiser, *Sister Carrie* (Philadelphia: University of Pennsylvania Press, 1981), 588–89.
    3. Conversation with Parker, Dec. 1983; see also n. 14 in *Flawed Texts and Verbal Icons*
(Chicago: Northwestern University Press, 1984), 6–7.

and change of "intention," or, in any case, of expression, are seriously curtailed in these editions.

Editing the "right" text, as conceived by an editor who is influenced by his particular formal orientation, may cause him to omit material he considers insignificant but that another scholar may consider important. Because there are different legitimate notions of when a work is finished and what aspects of its textual development are significant, the editor cannot smugly assert that his text is the best text. He must add a qualifier saying for what end or purpose his text is best. In recognizing the needs of scholars influenced by formal orientations differing from his own, the editor recognizes an obligation to provide an apparatus that will serve their needs as well as his own.

Chapter Seven

Ideal Texts

The term *ideal text* is frequently used among editors in two different senses, each a concern of this book. *Ideal,* contrasted to *real* or *actual,* is a term applicable to the notion that documents can misrepresent works. Thus, the work is "ideal," while documents are "real" (i.e., physical). This sense of the term permeates the arguments developed in chapters 3 through 5 and does not need to be rehearsed here. The primary arguments against the "existence" of such ideal texts are developed in chapter 8, "Critical Editions." The term ideal text also suggests a text that is ideal for some purpose—that is, a best text, in contrast to a corrupt or incomplete or damaged text. This use of the term can be applied to documents or to potential texts according to the orientation of the speaker.

Although the burden of my argument to this point has been that the scholar-critic will find useful and perhaps essential to his task of understanding the work of art something more than a single best text, whatever that might be, the concept of ideal text—a single, somehow best, or at least most adequate, representation of the work—is unavoidable in "the print era" because printed texts are linear. In a lecture on fiction Joyce Cary seemed to wish it otherwise but stated the irreducible "textual condition" forcefully when he said:

> It is quite true that language and the technique of the novel have their limitations. The most obvious is that of language, because language, unlike music, finds it difficult to say more than one thing at a time. A painter can give you the whole of his conception in one glance of an eye; the musician can convey very complex emotions simultaneously;

but the writer has to work in line, he has to say one thing after another. This is a very real limitation.[1]

The author's attempts to deal with the linearity of literary works include trial readings and revisions. From the author's point of view and that of commercial publishers, a single best text is undoubtedly the primary goal. Editors have almost always seen their roles as assistants in the author's quest for the ideal text—the text the author wished the public to have. Critics, for the most part, seem to act as if the book they are reading is that ideal text. The ideal text concept holds sway not only from reading habits based on unexamined assumptions but also because of the physical linearity of language, whether read or heard, that Cary described and lamented.

The concept of ideal (i.e., most appropriate single) text exists in two forms that together characterize perhaps 99 percent of the approaches to works of literary art. One, held by the great majority of critics, reflects what Hershel Parker describes as "the persistence of innocent trust in the text itself."[2] The sorry fact is that most critics begin with whatever text is at hand and trust that it is *the* text, never questioning whether it is ideal or not or else considering the issue unimportant. For them the text at hand is ideal because it is handy. The other form of the concept is held primarily by persons who claim to know the importance of scholarly editions. For them the ideal text is the text in its "final" or "most authoritative" form: the standard edition, the authorized edition, or the "definitive edition"— sometimes, though less and less, even the "definitive *text*." Critics who have been sensitized by stories of criticism based on "wrong" texts[3] ask for an ideal text to be edited and given to them as a fait accompli—a springboard, as it were, to the higher realms of criticism.[4]

---

1. Quoted from manuscript materials at the Bodleian Library by Melba Cuddy-Keane, "Joyce Cary's Working Papers: A Study of the Compositional Process in Narrative," *Journal of Modern Literature* 11 (July 1984): 320–21.

2. Parker, *Flawed Texts and Verbal Icons* (Chicago: Northwestern University Press, 1984), p. 231.

3. Note, for example, F. O. Matthiessen's "soiled fish" and F. R. Leavis on James's "mature" early texts. Gordon Ray, "The Importance of Original Editions," *Nineteenth Century English Books* (Urbana: University Illinois Press, 1952).

4. Much recent commentary on editorial theory has addressed positively the question of whether editing is a form of criticism and (persuasively) denies that editing is a precritical activity. See, particularly, *Textual Criticism and Literary Interpretation*, ed. Jerome J. McGann (Chicago: University of Chicago Press, 1985); and David Greetham, "Textual and Literary Theory: Redrawing the Matrix," *Studies in Bibliography* 42 (1989): 1–24; and "[Textual] Criticism and Deconstruction," *Studies in Bibliography*, 44 (1991): 1–30.

Editors also have a share in the concept of ideal text, and much of the bickering among editors over how to edit texts—what is the right theory of copy-text, what is the right emendation policy—results from conflicting notions of the ideal text of the work. Often the justification for a preference for one text over another ostensibly viable alternative text is that students and critics usually read only one text and do not use apparatuses, and, therefore, the clear-reading text should be the most authoritative or a standard text free of eccentricities as well as of errors. Arguments against alternative texts are often couched in pejorative terms such as *eccentric, mixed,* or *a text never seen or conceived before.* Nevertheless, under close examination these arguments turn out to be defenses for what a particular editor has convinced himself is the best single text of the work, the text he thinks the author would most have preferred to be remembered by, or the text through which, according to the editor, the author can or should best be understood.

In spite of the fact that in the 1980s editorial circles witnessed a paradigm shift in which the concept of a definitive end product was widely replaced by the concept of process in which multiple texts represent the work, nevertheless, the physical limitations of print editions and the linear reading habits of most readers have continued to force the predominance of clear-reading texts as a primary feature of new scholarly editions. Furthermore, hypertext multimedia editions, while very exciting to contemplate because they offer a triumph over the linear limitations of print editions through linked archives of texts, contexts, annotations, and criticism, do not triumph over the linear apprehension of texts. Though two or more texts may be simultaneously on a screen before the reader, simultaneous reading of alternate texts is not available to us as it might be in music. The electronic structure of the hypertext edition may no longer be linear, but to the reader it appears as multiple options through which to pick one's linear way. Hypertexts increase the ease with which readers can compare parts of one linear text with corresponding parts of others and with ancillary data, but they offer the opportunity for a meandering single (linear) path through works—a path that, once taken, may be very difficult to retrace, should one desire to do so. So, even with hypertexts, the question of "a best text for some purpose" will remain very much with us. In view of the human limits to assimilate "nonlinear" texts (as opposed to the physical limitations of print or the mechanical dexterity of electronic media), the most important point arising from recent theoretical discussions and computer capabilities may be the inescapable recognition by the general reader that any reading text is merely representative of a work, not "the work itself"; for there are other representations of it crowding in demanding attention as well.[5] This double need for a single text and a sense of its inadequacy seems evident not just in spite of the arguments of the bibliographic orientation (that each book is, in a sense, the work incarnate, uniquely and inevitably)[6] but also because of these arguments, for it seems inescapable that the particularity, the uniqueness, of the physical entities of texts renders each no more than one of various representations of the work demanding attention in other forms as well.

Be that as it may, for print editions and the coming electronic editions, one of the continuing basic questions of editorial work is: what is the ideal text? The one that will be read? The one that will be the clear-reading text of the new edition? The one that will stand first in the electronic menu of available texts? The one that will be spun off in paperback from the electronic archive? In posing that question the editor might also be asking: what is the most complete text? The clearest? The most effective? The most unified? The one with the purest textual integrity? Put in this way, these questions sound like reflections of the aesthetic orientation, but each of these questions can be put in terms compatible with any of the five orientations I have discussed. It is important to ask the question about ideal text and the bases for its identification, because it forces us to explore, in ways not often thoroughly pursued, the processes of creation, revision, and "editing" by the author and the course of the artist's reactions to external influences. In turn, this exercise forces us to assess how important we think such investigations are in critical responses to the work of art. To carry out this exploration effectively we must look at the work once more from the author's point of view, asking what kinds of revisions and alterations were made, what circumstances and motives influenced the changes, and how cognizant the author was of the effect that revisions have on unrevised parts of the text.[7]

---

5. Murray McGillivray, ("Towards a Post-Critical Edition: Theory, Hypertext, and the Presentation of Middle English Wroks," *Text* 7 [1994]: 175–99) makes this point as well, though he begins with an attack on critical editing as a violation of the integrity of historical documents. The result of the archival alternative is too daunting for him, however, and he admits that there is a need for critically edited texts.

6. C. Deirdre Phelps ("The Edition as Art Form in Textual and Interpretive Criticism," *Text* 7 [1994], 69) argues the position effectively, saying, "A book's particular combination, say, of morocco binding, small pica type, hot-press paper, and colored plates is not a version of any other possible combination, but is unique and complete as an expression of its momentary fabrication."

7. In posing the editorial task in these terms, I am conscious of Hershel Parker's similar

To explore this question is to ascertain why it was both funny and serious when an author friend of mine announced one day, "Well, I've just finished my novel—again." The exploration may help us understand why editors, critics, authors, and publishers usually think of works of literary art as one text, and it will help focus attention on ways in which editors can best serve the users of scholarly editions. (I return to this question also in chap. 10 "Copy-texts and Apparatuses.")

The key to this exploration is to identify the role of an editor's literary critical stance in the editing process. Let us begin by returning to the earliest point in editorial theory at which critical preferences lead editors into disagreement: the concept of authority. When authority is defined, a net is created through which all nonauthoritative variants fall to the editorial workshop floor. The net harvests all authoritative forms of the work. From these forms the edited text of the work can emerge.

The net created by a strictly documentary and by the bibliographic definition of authority is solid; no individual variants fall through it, for documentary authority equates the authoritative document with the authoritative form of the text. The most this net can do is sift out nonauthoritative documents. And, because the bibliographic orientation equates the work with each bibliographically distinct instance of it, each document has a distinct authority.

The net created by the authorial definition of authority will catch only those variants that originated with the author and, sometimes, other variants that the author sanctioned. When the origin or sanction of a variant is indeterminate, that variant is called indifferent. One of the things that is meant by "critical" editing is the exercise of critical choices to resolve "indifferent" variants—to decide whether or not a particular variant or class of variants was caught by the net or allowed to fall through.

But a further task awaits the editor who has sifted out nonauthoritative readings. What remains in the net includes alternative readings—variants between what was authoritative at different times or for different forms of publication. Nonauthoritative forms, by definition, have no place in the work, but all authoritative forms, by definition, do have a place in the work—that which is implied by the variant authoritative forms of the work. In much editorial discussion, however, the concept of authority, once it has separated the authoritative from the nonauthoritative textual forms, is carried forward to help resolve the problems of choosing among alternate

---

appeal (*Flawed Texts and Verbal Icons,* 182), though I think mine is an observation of a state of being, not a polemical appeal for editors to "come over" (242).

authoritative readings. But to carry the concept of authority forward for this purpose is to confuse thinking by making one term apply to two different things. The concept of authority is crucial for separating authoritative forms from nonauthoritative forms but is inappropriate, if not useless, as a tool to distinguish among the authoritative forms in order to create or select the ideal text to be the clear reading text of the new edition.

Fredson Bowers was careful to point out that, when an author revises his work, the new words, which are authoritative, do not deprive the old words of their authority.[8] He was clearly aware that a principle for choosing among authoritative forms is needed if an editor is to produce a clear-reading text, and he offered a principle for selecting what he called the forms with "superior" authority. But he did not distinguish by name between the principle for identifying authority and the principle for choosing among the differing authoritative readings, nor did he acknowledge that his system for selecting the superior authority is grounded in the literary critical theory he espouses. That is to say, Bowers acted as though his notion of the best text, judged critically to be so, coincided with the last text the author produced. Though each reading produced by the author is authoritative, the last authoritative reading has "superior authority." By calling it superior authority, Bowers avoided calling it the "best text," but he clearly thought of it as the best text. The reason he did not acknowledge the extent of the critical foundation for his preference may be that he assumed that everyone agreed with his conception of ideal texts, which is to incorporate "final authorial intention."[9] As long as everyone agrees on that point, there is no problem with Bowers's method of identifying superior authority. But not everyone does agree.

And so, the distinction between authoritative and nonauthoritative is not a useful tool for selecting the ideal text from among the competing authorial variants. The only tool that *is* useful for this selection process is a frankly critical one. It involves the editor's notion of *what* the work of art

---

8. Presidential address, Society for Textual Scholarship, New York, Apr., 1985.

9. Bowers always called his kind of editing "critical" because the editor uses critical judgment in acting upon indifferent variants and because eclectic editing involves the application of argued principles to the problem of selecting the readings that represent the author's final intentions even when the copy-text was the earliest available document. This is not the same as admitting that a preference for the author's final intentions is itself critically based. See Bowers's article "Authorial Intention and Editorial Problems," *Text* 5 (1991): 49–61, for his analysis of an example of identifying final authorial intention in an instance in which there are conflicting authorial intentions and outside intervention in the texts. See also my comments on that argument in "Textual Variants, Performance Variants, and the Concept of Work," *Editio: Internationales Jahrbuch for Editionswissenschaft* 7 (1993): 221–34, esp. 226–28.

is. According to one authorial intentionalist school, it is the last thing the author did—unless he can be shown to have acted under a "nonartistic" influence. For another intentionalist it is what the author did while in the grip of the creative impulse, which is the center of the author's authority. This is a text that can be identified only by checking the coherence of the work as a whole as understood by the most comprehensive and responsible critical methods—as understood by the editor. For the sociological school it includes the conventionalizing influence of an authorized publication process. It seems to me that debatable critical preferences are involved in the definition of authority and that criticism is involved again when a selection among authoritative alternatives is made.

Like editors of any other orientation toward authority, documentary editors face the problem of choosing among authoritative forms after the nonauthoritative have been screened out. They must decide which authoritative document to reproduce. And, as with the authorial editors choosing among the author's alternative texts, documentary editors' choices are made on grounds other than authority, for they are choosing among documents of competing authority. Their choice is made on critical grounds: which is the best or most appropriate document? It is important to examine the grounds for the choice made here, for, traditionally, the documentary orientation is thought of as the most conservative, most objective, editorial approach, the one that eliminates most thoroughly the editor's exercise of critical preference. But even here we see critical preferences with sweeping effects on any reader's experience of the text.

It can be argued that bibliographical and paleographical evidence resolves many textual problems without recourse to critical principles. If one discounts the critical element in the definition of authority, this is true. Evidence revealing the chronology of textually variant forms or the source of the variant can lead to undisputable conclusions about many specific problems. All of the bibliographical work and all the normal tools of editorial investigation continue to be necessary in order to establish the chronology and sources of textual change. Evidence demonstrating that a nonauthoritative person is the source of an alteration deprives that alteration of a place in the work. Censorship is usually treated by authorial and aesthetic editors as nonauthoritative. When the evidence is ambiguous about the source, an "indifferent" situation exists. A critical act is required to select one alternative for the reading text and the other for a place in the apparatus. (It is even a critical act to resolve indifferent cruxes by resorting to the copy-text, for it affects the reader's experience of the text.) When the source is not in question and the chronology is established, a critical act of a different order is necessary in selecting the ideal reading. Critics react to alternative authoritative readings by pondering alternative meanings or alternative effects. They are less likely to react this way to indifferent variants—those that could be, but are not known to be, authoritative. And they certainly do not ponder in this way the alternatives offered by nonauthoritative variants. But, of course, the question of what readings are authoritative depends on the critic's orientation toward forms. The critic interested in authorially intended meanings will be irritated by texts riddled with nonauthorial interventions; the critic interested in the social processes of text creation will be irritated by texts "tampered with" by a modern editor's efforts to restore authorial forms.

Claims to the contrary by editors of great and small reputation notwithstanding, the principles for selection among authoritative variants in order to create a single reading text reflect values that emanate from the editor's critical preferences and acknowledged or unacknowledged aesthetic principles. That is to say, choices among authoritative forms of the text are in no sense scientific or objective. This is a fact to be acknowledged, not a weakness or flaw in any editorial theory. But nearly all scholarly editors abhor this fact and quite desperately develop theories and principles of editing designed to control individuality of choice and its much feared potential for editorial eccentricity. Editors are always careful to justify as principled and objective the editorial choices they must make.

I am not now conflating all scholarly editing into one editorial orientation, the aesthetic. Unlike the other three, the aesthetic orientation acknowledges the editor's critical basis for creating the ideal text, but it assumes for the editor an uninhibited authority to create the ideal text on the editor's own aesthetic principles. This view should not be confused with the principles of commercial editing usually prevailing with literary agents and publishers trying to forge a best text for commercial purposes. The aesthetic principle as it appears in scholarly editing may resemble commercial tastes, but it usually restricts its range of improving emendations to the variants already found in authoritative sources, severely limiting the number and type of speculative emendations designed to correct apparent lapses where no extant variant seems satisfactory. This view is distinguished also from authorial orientations that attempt to preserve the notion of alternative authorial versions of the work distinct from one another because of differing intended audiences for differing publications or by significant lapses of time between revisions or by palpable changes of mind about what the work should say. The aesthetic orientation not only picks critically among the authoritative documents; it picks eclectically among the versions to create a single best text.

One way to understand what distinguishes the other orientations from the aesthetic is the nature of the inhibitions to editorial activity imposed by their definitions of authority, which tend to deprive the editor of a free hand. Insofar as these principles make editing appear to be precise or objective, they can be seen as providing scholarly rigor to the editing profession. But, when this idea is carried too far, as it quite often very clearly has been, it makes editing appear to be a mechanical procedure that can be "done right." If editing can be done "right" and nearly "mechanically," then it can probably best be done by unimaginative pedants and drudges. That this view of things is both naive and dangerous need hardly be argued, for the critical significance of editorial choices can be demonstrated with every scholarly edition produced. And yet most literary critics continue to exercise their "high calling" on a single text (often, unfortunately, on any old single text), testimony to the general failure of both critics and editors to realize the tremendous importance of the critical and imaginative element of scholarly editing.

Therefore, when it is said that an editor "should prefer" a certain choice between authoritative variants, this must be understood to mean that, if a person shares certain critical values, whatever they may be, about authority for texts, then that particular choice should be preferred. T. H. Howard-Hill provides a very interesting example of how an editor, working within a well-defined authorial orientation, carefully weighing the evidence and developing as airtight as possible an argument leading to an editorial choice, can conclude with confidence that an editor "should prefer" a reading from a printed text of uncertain authority over a reading found in two manuscripts in the author's hand.[10] Howard-Hill makes three interesting distinctions: first, between variations introduced by the author and those introduced by others; second, between variations resulting from genuine attempts to improve the play through revision and careless errors and omissions (Middleton is described as a "barely competent" scribe [308]); and, third, between revisions developing *A Game at Chess* as a *play* (a stage production shaped to conform to political and stage exigencies at the time of performance) and those developing it as a *work* (a printed contribution to

---

10. T. H. Howard-Hill, "The Author as Scribe or Reviser? Middleton's Intentions in *A Game at Chess*," *Text* 3 (1987): 308–18, esp. 314.

the literature of the nation).[11] These distinctions are crucial in illustrating my point that agreement with an editor's conclusions depends upon sharing a fundamental critical orientation toward texts. The manuscripts, both scribal and authorial, appear to have been written out as prepublication means of circulating the play to acquire patronage. If that is the case, then a published version (Q1), ostensibly composed from a no-longer-extant manuscript prepared by Middleton, would supersede these extant manuscripts in certain ways. These ways cannot be specified very precisely, however, because it is also possible that Q1 includes mistakes or compositorial lapses and sophistications. To illustrate his point, that the printed text has greater authority than extant authorial manuscripts, Howard-Hill points to one passage where, in the manuscripts, captured chess pieces are thrown into the "pitt," a word with obviously hellish connotations, but the printed text (Q1) has them thrown into the "bag," a word closer to the prevailing chess game metaphor and the word used every other time in the scene. Howard-Hill concludes: "The Q1 variation of 'bag' [f]or 'pitt' develops the author's intention and is a reading which an editor, despite its absence from the two manuscripts written in the dramatist's hand, should prefer in an edition" (314). That there is a choice between *pitt* and *bag* is undeniably supported by bibliographical evidence, yet Howard-Hill's choice of *bag* seems to me clearly "critical," both because it is a choice between two readings, each of which has a claim to authority, and because his editorial orientation is based on a critical preference for an author's final intentions and not a preference for documentary integrity or social collaborations or aesthetic taste. Only if one adopts Howard-Hill's orientation toward works and, in particular, his theory that Q1 was based on copy specifically prepared for publication would one say that his conclusion "should be preferred."

Another editor, also pursuing authorial intention but assessing the evidence differently, might prefer *pitt* because it is in Middleton's handwriting. The editor of the New Mermaids Series edition of *A Game at Chess* did prefer *pitt* without saying why; he did not even record the fact that *bag* was an alternative. It could easily be argued that the manuscript's *pitt* is the superior reading, since it adds an appropriate dimension to the scene, whereas *bag* is already overused. The point is that the grounds for the choice, regardless of the exhaustiveness of research and the meticulousness

---

11. In this article Howard-Hill forgoes the opportunity to have fun with the terms *work* and *play*, especially in reference to a text called *A Game* . . . .

of the arguments, have ceased, in the richness of conflicting and ambiguous evidence, to be the concept of authority and are basically critical. The sociological, documentary, and bibliographical orientations would all agree with Howard-Hill's choice of *bag*, but none would do so for his reasons. They would, furthermore, reject entirely his eclectic melding of readings from several documents into an edited text. Some would argue that their disagreements with Howard-Hill are based on the fact that his method is essentially interpretive criticism, while theirs is more objective. That is not the case. The consequences of their editorial choice of Q1 (if that were the base text for their edition) would entail all the critically interpretive choices made by the agents of its production. Shifting the action from their own editorial shoulders to those of the original production crews by one sweeping decision to accept what those crews did does not diminish the critical consequences of that choice. It is not an objective choice; it is critical. It is not a criticism of scholarly editing to point out that editions are critically constructed through many points of choice that could be determined by different editors in different ways. It does, however, indicate both the extreme intellectual delicacy of editorial work and the sweeping effects editing has on readers' experiences of the work.

Although it now passes as a commonplace, it took me a long time to figure out the extent of criticism in editing, because in most discussions of editorial work the emphasis was on rejecting critical aesthetic principles in favor of "objective" theories and principles for creating standard, or "definitive," editions. Recognizing the critical foundation for editorial work makes perfect sense out of what is otherwise puzzling, frustrating, or even paralyzing to the editor. It reveals why editors sometimes hate to do what their principles require them to do. It explains why there are disagreements among editors about what the ideal text of a work should be or about how a particular work should be edited. For a time our most respected and influential teachers led us to believe that the principles of copy-text and emendation are sufficiently well established and flexible to accommodate the differences in methodology demanded by differing textual situations.

When it became in the 1980s commonly remarked that scholarly editions attempting to establish authorial intentions were works of interpretive criticism, movement away from the so-called Bowers school of critical editing gained momentum. It consisted of a swing toward the bibliographical and sociological orientations, each of which claims to be less interpretive and more historical than the authorial, or "intentionalist," school of editing.

When McGann began his revolt against the Greg/Bowers principles, we were told he did not sufficiently understand the applicability of those principles to the cases he was studying. His rebellion, however, seems to have arisen from his attempts to apply to Lord Byron's works principles of copy-text and emendation that were based on a concept of authority preventing him from admitting to the text readings that, as critic, he believed to be necessary for an ideal production of the work. I do not know if he would put it that way. I put it that way as my analysis of the disagreement between McGann's and Bower's approaches to the "textual situation" to emphasize that the literary critical values of these theorists are fundamental to their choices of readings for edited texts. Because the net defined by authorial authority eliminated readings essential to the text he wanted to produce, McGann redefined authority, creating a net that would hold alterations introduced by the production crews that first transmitted manuscript text to printed text.[12] This expedient served his needs and those of other like-minded editors so well that his definition of authority quickly gained the status of an alternative to the Greg/Bowers editorial school. McGann is, in fact, reported to have announced (prematurely, I should add) the death of the "copy-text school of scholarly editing" at the 1991 "Palimpsest" conference on editing.[13]

Based on a principle that appears objective—authority resides in the institution of publishing represented in published editions—McGann's approach seems to require admittance into the work readings that to some editors seem inappropriately intrusive and that offend their own critical assessments of the work. The concept of authority McGann developed to deal with texts by Byron even gives him trouble, as he himself readily demonstrates in his treatment of Shelley's texts. Furthermore, it leaves him apparently paralyzed when he is faced with an unpublished work with variant manuscript forms, none of which has been given ideal form by an authoritative socializing institution. Two keys releasing editors from the tyranny of their own theories are recognition of the multiple nature of literary texts and of the fundamentally critical nature of editorial theories. Fortunately, McGann's is not the only alternative to the Greg/Bowers formula.

When Bowers and Tanselle distinguished between an author's "last" intentions and his "final" intentions, they revealed a fundamental feature of

---

12. McGann drew heavily upon, or at least echoed largely, the approaches to editing that had been proposed by James Thorpe and Philip Gaskell. This historical background gave his expedient popular impetus. See also chapter 3, n. 1.

13. W. Speed Hill, review of *Papers from "New Directions in Textual Studies,"* in *Text* 6 (1994): 370.

their emendation principles that is nonmechanical, nonautomatic, nonobjective. As long as it appeared that last intentions equaled final intentions, the authorial definition of authority seemed an unerring and nearly mechanical guide to choosing the "superior" authority among the competing authoritative forms of the text. A mechanical choice has the advantage over any other in that it appears to be objective and inevitable, not subjective and tentative. But when *final* meant the rejection of chronologically last revisions whenever these were judged to be coerced or nonartistic, an aesthetically based principle was invoked to distinguish between artistic and nonartistic revisions; in such cases the editor's critical faculties were not restricted to use in deciding how to deal with indifferent variants but were used also in selecting among the alternative authoritative variants. The principle of selection thus revealed is based squarely on a critical opinion about what the author was, or should have been, trying to do.

Parker accuses most recent editors of American literature of betraying, though often not acknowledging, a New Critical bias, which assumes that unity is one of the central aims (intentions?) of any work of art. As applied by the "Bowers school" to the editorial choice among authoritative variants, forms that disrupt unity are said either to have been imposed on the author by external influence rather than motivated by artistic impulses or to have merely the appearance of disrupting unity. Parker first recognizes the critical bases (and biases) for much modern American editorial work (in spite of protestations to the contrary) and then rejects, as too narrowly based, the critical principles that informed those editorial goals. In their place he offers a more widely based psycho-socio-biographical-historical-textual-critical foundation and carries to its logical conclusion a boldly critical approach to editing. He sees the author himself in some cases as an external force when he continues to "edit" his own work after authority over it has passed out of his control. The trouble with Parker's position is that, as with Bowers's, one must agree with a critical opinion about what the text should be. Neither readily admitted to disagreements. Bowers seemed to argue that his position was right because it was bibliographical (hence objective) and not critical. That is not true. Parker seems to argue that his position is right because it takes into account all the historical, social, biographical, and psychological considerations that he finds essential to responsible literary criticism. Bowers's position seems deceptive (the critical, nonobjective, element is hidden in order to make the result seem more perfect and persuasive), or it is naive (not recognizing the nonobjective element and believing that no viable alternative exists). Parker's position, because it frankly acknowledges the critical element in its foundation, seems far more sophisticated and useful, but it seems to claim too much for itself—too much confidence in the correctness or inevitability of the critical principles involved.

Every carefully thought out and elaborated theory and practice of editing, because it must be elaborated within a coherent notion of the nature of works and authority, is bound to conflict with the theories and practices of editors working within other orientations. It is perhaps legitimate within a single paradigm to identify arguments as illogical or practice as inconsistent with theory, but to claim to have reached conclusions that everyone must prefer or to condemn a theory or practice because it does not conform to one's own fundamental notions seems silly.

If, as I have argued, the various editorial orientations are elaborate attempts to control the exercise of an editor's critical activity but that, instead, succeed primarily in disguising that activity, what alternatives does the editor actually face? Should he admit as a fundamental truth that editing is a form of literary criticism in which the editor's critical standards, biases, and commitments are reflected in the resulting "ideal" text? Or should he set about to find an editorial principle that really and truly *does* eliminate the critical element from his work? The basic problem arises from the confrontation of the linear nature of physical texts and the notion that works are essentially either multiple rather than singular or that the ideal text is extractable from multiple documentary forms only by the exercise of critical selections. The appeal of "objective" editorial criteria has always been that an individual editor's choices should not be foisted onto the public. The difficulty is that the only way to present a work with a multiple form is in a multiple text—that is, not a linear text.

From 1976, when Todd Bender began writing about the feasibility of the electronic books with variant texts stacked in a three-dimensional field on a computer screen[14] until the present, when hypertexts and multimedia have begun to take practical shape,[15] the objectivity of an archival

14. Todd Bender, "Literary Texts in Electronic Storage: The Editorial Potential," *Computers and the Humanities* 10 (1976): 193–99, and "Stable vs. Unstable Intention in Conrad: The View from the Database," Society for Textual Scholarship Convention, New York, Apr. 1985.
15. See Peter L. Shillingsburg,"Polymorphic, Polysemic, Protean, Reliable Electronic Texts," in *Palimpsest: Editorial Theory in the Humanities,* ed. George Bornstein and Ralph G. Williams (Ann Arbor: University of Michigan Press, 1993), 29–43; and J. J. McGann, *The Rationale of Hypertext* (posted on World Wide Web: http://jefferson.village.virginia.edu/ [under General Publications]).

approach to text presentation has been appealing. It makes the "multiple work" available in its multiple forms simultaneously, and it appears to eliminate the editor's critical orientation except as it is involved in excluding nonauthoritative source texts. But it has two significant drawbacks that belie this appeal. First, it is questionable if any reader can read two, three, or more texts simultaneously. Even if a reader could do that, what would he or she be reading?—variant texts of documents. Many manuscripts and most printed documents represent a point at which the process of writing has stopped, like a snapshot. Each document cooperatively, collaboratively, or mere jointly produced represents mixed authority. A second drawback is that an electronic archive of documents would not be an array of variant versions of a work, unless some editorial work were done to make the "stacked texts" be more accurate representations of authorial or other ideal (i.e., not documentary) versions.[16] In a work by Thackeray, for example, the array of documentary texts thus displayed would submerge the significant authorial variations in a sea of insignificant compositorial ones. On the other hand, any attempt to stack a sequence of authorial versions would require "editing out" of the text of each documentary version the nonauthoritative elements—that would require, in turn, a definition of authority, and every definition of authority involves a literary critical aesthetic.

Another possibility for eliminating the editor's critical involvement by truly representing a multiple-form work in a multiple text is demonstrated by Michael J. Warren's *Complete King Lear*.[17] The competing authoritative quartos and folio are reproduced in facsimile in toto, and two basic variant texts are to be edited in parallel form with further variant forms indicated in marginalia. The editor's critical preference for one, or more, texts is subordinated to the arrangement of competing documentary textual forms. Each reader will have the opportunity to sort through the material, weigh the options, and, in a sense, either edit his own ideal text or perhaps succeed in holding in his mind the variant forms and enrich his understanding of the whole work by somehow contemplating simultaneously the variant

---

16. Some editors would consider this an advantage, not a drawback, because they see an array of documents as objective, where an array of versions as I've defined them would be subjective. My arguments are that an array of documents is just as subjective as an array of versions and that readers have legitimate reasons for wanting both.

17. Described by Warren in "The Problem of Multiple Texts and the Complete *King Lear*," Society for Textual Scholarship Convention, New York, Apr. 1985; Michael Warren and Gary Taylor *The Division of the Kingdom: Shakespeare's Two Versions of King Lear* (Oxford: Clarendon Press, 1983); and *The Complete "King Lear"*, ed. Warren (Berkeley: University of California Press, 1989).

texts that imply the work. It is difficult to describe what this reading experience will be without betraying some vagueness of concept and potential for confusion.

But to opt for a single self-sufficient and adequate ideal text conceived as the product of objective scholarship is to revert to naïveté or deception. The only real alternative to a multiple, nonlinear text for scholarly editions is the creation of an ideal text based on frankly acknowledged critical principles—reflecting a clearly conceived and well-articulated editorial orientation that presents *text* and *process* as equally important parts of the edited work of art. To do that successfully, the process or progression of authoritative forms must be presented (in a textual apparatus or electronic archive) in useful and easily accessible form, separate from other compilations of textual and bibliographical evidence that may be necessary for other reasons.

Such edited texts will not be definitive, any more than any other product of literary criticism is definitive. The word *definitive* should be banished from editorial discussion. Scholarly editions can be no more than valuable access routes to the work of art. Critics will learn how to use scholarly editions when they stop mistaking the clear-reading text of a scholarly edition for the work itself and when they stop regarding the textual apparatus as a repository of discarded and superseded variants preserved by pompous pedants. When critics will learn that, I cannot guess, since many editors who should know better have yet to learn it. Editors will stop deceiving themselves and their publics when they acknowledge that there are no objective procedures for editing texts and that the texts they produce are influenced by their critically based orientations and insights. There is no mechanically pure method of producing sound texts.

There is, of course, an objective way to record the differences in the texts preserved in the authoritative documents. What is often called the "bibliographic" evidence of "textual transmission" can be assembled—and must be assembled by any editor who is trying to find out the basic facts about the work being editing. A full historical collation is an objective representation of the documentary history of textual transmission. The succession of potential ideal texts representing authorial versions of the work, however, does not necessarily equal the succession of texts preserved in documents. The record, therefore, of the composition and revision and alteration that is authoritative (and, hence, useful in literary criticism) must be separated from the fuller record that is documentary and bibliographical (and, hence, useful to students of publishing history and the manufacture of books). There is no objective principle for identifying the versions of the work—not even the final one. Nevertheless, many editors congratulate themselves on applying standard methodologies with scholarly rigor in order to produce scholarly editions, relying on the orthodoxy of the method to ensure the quality of the resulting text. The banishment of criticism from the editorial arena has made editors think that, if the method is right, the text will be right, whether or not it makes sense. Whether editors like it or not, the ideal texts they produce reflect their critical acumen. Perhaps that is why editing is held in low esteem by the profession at large. Perhaps that is why writing a critical book counts for more in the race for promotion than editing a text. At least the author of a critical book accepts responsibility for the coherence of his work. Editors *are* critics, too; an edition reflects the editor's critical biases and talent or lack thereof. Editors are responsible for the coherence of the product, not just for the rigor of the methodology.

Therefore, edition users have a very high stake in knowing what principles were used to produce the edition they are relying on, and they should take a keen interest in how the apparatus reports the alternative authoritative forms of the work.

It may be noticed that in this chapter on ideal texts I have not tried to specify how I think ideal texts should be edited. This is deliberate. My method has its own critical foundation, and, while I find it convincing enough for me, it is not the only method that can be cogently defended. The burden of this chapter has, instead, been on three points. The first is that editors will, or should, acknowledge freely the critical foundation of the principles leading them to their ideal texts, which are tentative and not definitive. The second is that, by understanding the critical nature of their own principles better, editors will be freer to act according to their lights when their principles seem to lead them astray—making them do what their critical senses tell them is wrong. And the third is that editors will, or should, redesign their apparatuses to reflect the work and its alternative authoritative forms in easily accessible ways, so that the emphasis of the apparatus is not on what the editor did or on what the bibliographical and documentary evidence is.

A further discussion of the presentation of an edition and of the equal importance of *text* and *process* appears in chapter 10 ("Copy-Texts and Apparatuses").

Chapter Eight

Critical Editions

The term *critical edition* has become as problematic as the term *ideal text*. A brief survey of the range of definitions it serves will help initiate a mapping of its various uses and reveal the grounds of contention.

When extant manuscripts, proofs, and books for a work are analyzed and arranged in a stemma or family tree to indicate the lines of descent from the original inscription of the work, it is often apparent that some links in the line are missing. For ancient works it is most often the original inscription and perhaps many descendants from it that are missing, preceding our now extant most ancient document. In such cases editors traditionally have attempted to reconstruct a missing link or the archetype by inferring the readings it might have had from the patterns of variant readings that do exist. One definition declares critical editing to be the process of reconstructing now lost texts.

When a work exists in only one surviving document, an editor may undertake to identify and correct textual flaws. Such flaws are identifiable by their violation of conventions such as orthography or grammar, by their awkward scansion or missed rhyme, or by the editor's failure to make sense of the text as found in the document. Another definition, therefore, declares critical editing to be the process of identifying and correcting errors or stylistic lapses in the text being edited. Obviously, this procedure is also applicable to works for which multiple texts exist, but it is called to bear most purely in this sense when only one text survives or when all extant texts agree in the apparently erroneous reading.

Scholarly editorial work before this century was mostly confined to ancient texts represented by unique copies or only by scribal copies. It is clear, therefore, why critical editing has traditionally been defined in these two ways. Although there is no reason to believe that ancient writers did not revise their works or produce differing versions for differing audiences, there is little or no surviving evidence of such activity. Variations in surviving documents have usually been assumed, therefore, to result from scribal ineptness or sophistication, not authorial revision. The modern editorial task for ancient works, then, has been to reconstruct the text as it must originally have been. It has been normal to think of that original as one text.

When editors turned to modern texts, they encountered situations never dreamed of by biblical and classical editors: the existence of multiple original documents in which the work of the author and of secretaries, editors, and compositors could be identified. The stemma became a means to sort out the richness of materials rather than a preliminary measure to redress the paucity of authoritative evidence. Of course, it was not always possible to identify the source or authority of variant readings; textual materials for modern works is also frequently missing. So, the principles of critical reconstruction were adapted. The richness of materials, however, brought new choices between early and late authoritative, even authorial, publications; between magazine, newspaper, and book publications; between serial editions, first editions, and revised editions—each of which had the potential to reflect a different intention for the work. It was no longer clearly the case that the editorial goal was to recover a lost original document. It became possible with modern texts to formulate a new goal: constructing not the text of a lost document but, instead, that of a lost original opportunity for a text that never actually came into existence. Authorial intention, distinguished from the accidents and ineptitudes of text production, became a possible editorial option. So, another definition emerged, declaring critical editing to be the process of extracting from the plethora of authoritative evidence an intended text not yet realized. Needless to say, editors who object to the intentionalist school of editing object to this use of the term *critical editing*.

The primary goal of the first type of editing is the *reconstruction* of the text of a lost document. The primary goal of the second order is the *polishing,* or *purification,* of an existing text. And the primary goal of the third is the *construction* of a new text from a plethora of extant materials, each authoritative but deemed corrupt or damaged in some way. Given a specific case, many editors would employ all three types of editing. But the documentary, bibliographical, and sociological editors would tend to emphasize reconstruction, go very lightly with polishing, and reject construction. The authorial orientation, with its emphasis on intention, would attempt to reconstruct a lost document only to the degree to which it led to a better understanding of what the author intended and would rely heavily on constructing a new text—but would tend to call it a *re*construction or *re*storation.

One thing most editors will agree about is that all three types of editing involve the exercise of critical judgment and, hence, could be called critical editing. Most would also agree that the term critical editing applies, whether an editor chooses to produce an emended text representing the critically derived or corrected text or chooses only to indicate those forms in notes or an apparatus for a text that faithfully reproduces its source.

Because editing in the mid-twentieth century was confronted with a type of material editors had not faced before, offering opportunities to pursue editorial ends not possible to contemplate before, it is not surprising that new principles for editing arose, bringing with them turmoil and dissension. A field of study that had legitimated itself for centuries by emphasizing its empirical methodology was rocked by the discovery that its work was unavoidably interpretive. Much of the debate about editorial procedure can be understood as an attempt to return editing to its roots, to define critical editing as it had been before the advent of Greg, Bowers, and interpretive editing, and to focus editorial efforts on the preservation and understanding of history rather than on redressing its wrongs. I do not think such attempts will or should succeed *at the expense of intentionalist editing.*[1] Properly understood, there is no reason not to have both types of editing. Indeed, I believe the profession will soon see that we cannot do without both and that neither is very satisfactory. In the meantime, however, the debate has been very salutary in focusing the attention of the editing world on the implications of various procedures. Certainly, much of the backlash against the intentionalist school arises from its early exaggerated claims of definitiveness. No one seriously claims that editing can be done definitively. And, recently, the intentionalist's claims to adequacy, combined with their habit of dealing primarily, if not exclusively, with the

---

1. In *Text* 7 (1994), essays by McGann, McGillevray, Higdon and Harper, and Hunt either warn against the evils of eclectic editing or tout the adequacy of textual archives where critical constructions are no longer necessary. See also Morris Eaves, "'Why Don't They Leave It Alone?' Speculations on the Authority of Audience in Editorial Theory," in *Cultural Artifacts and the Production of Meaning: The Page, the Image, and the Body,* ed. Margaret J. M. Ezell and Katherine O'Brien O'Keeffe (Ann Arbor: University of Michigan Press, 1994) 85–99.

linguistic code of texts, has drawn hostile fire. But the desire to be objective or to curb sharply interpretive and subjective editorial acts is still strong and seems a motivating force for some of the attacks on intentionalist, or "copy-text," editing. But growing awareness of orientations other than the authorial and of needs not met by intentionalist editions will not, should not, replace the distinctive advantages of eclectic editions.

The rawest edge of contention over this principle is currently waged over the issue of versions—over whether *versions* are coeval with *documents* and whether *authorship* is coeval with *authority*. These two principles are extremely important in the developing argument because these issues deeply affect editorial theory and practice. One way to understand what is at stake in this argument is to focus on the editorial and interpretive question: is one interpreting and editing textual documents (material texts produced by one or multiple authorities), or is one interpreting and editing textual voices (intended texts embedded, ineptly or purely, by one writer alone or in conjunction with others in extant documentary texts).

One side of the idea of editorial theory argues as follows:[2]

1. One should begin with the fact that physical documents (manuscripts, proofs, editions) are extant and relatively stable. One can make positive, verifiable, accurate statements about them. Most disputes over what a documentary text "says" (i.e., disputes about the letters and punctuation of which it consists) can be settled or remain local, specific problems. Physical documents are the sine qua non of the textual condition.[3]

2. The textual condition is material, and the production of material texts occurs in a materialist world. This claim has its foundations in Marxist theory, and certainly there is important truth in the idea that a materialist/economic system has a great deal to do with how texts are created and what texts say: authors cannot say in texts things that cannot be represented in linguistic or iconic signs on paper; authors seldom deliberately say things that

---

2. What follows is a redaction of a "side" of the idea supported by textual critics as diverse as Jack Stillinger, Jerome McGann, Randall McLoed, James Thorpe, Donald Pizer, Hans Gabler, and Morris Eaves. I say diverse, because they do not agree about the implications of these views.

3. Since the publication of McGann's essay and book titled *The Textual Condition* the phrase has attached itself to his view of that condition: that texts are documentary, bibliographic, and social—and hence not extractable into distinctions between "the text of the document" and "the text of the work." His view is irreconcilably opposed to the view that the "real" text is always liable to be misrepresented by its material media.

would be censored or cause their works to remain unpublished or unpurchased;[4] and texts have a commodity status that influences their linguistic composition as well as their material production.

3. Textual authority is social. For the production and final shaping of their works, authors usually enter agreements with publishing institutions that have traditions and conventions concerning the production of works. Therefore, it seems reasonable to say that the results of production processes, the material texts, accurately represent the shared authority indemic to the textual condition.

4. The most apparent result of thinking in these ways is the tendency to equate versions of the work with documents of the work. The attraction of this view is that disputes over *version* can be anchored, in the same way as disputes over *text*, in the physical document. The most compelling argument in favor of this conclusion, however, is the unattractiveness of alternatives to it.

If one adopts Tanselle's (and others') contention that the documentary text may *mis*represent the intended version, that neither the version or the work inheres in the physical document, then one is an idealist. Idealists are committed by their belief in the corruptibility of physical documents to the notion that editors and readers have a responsibility to find or posit a nonextant text as the accurate representation of the version. But how is that done? For advocates of the materialist view of versions, the answers to that question indicate what is unacceptable and unattractive about the idealist view.

1. Tanselle contends that typos are regularly recognized, corrected, and discounted by readers. It is clear, therefore, that readers regularly act as though the intended text should be *derived* from the physical text and, hence, is not coeval with the physical texts. But Stillinger points out that not all typos are in fact recognized as such, some so-called typos are not in fact typos at all, and when typos are recognized and corrected they are not always corrected in the same way.[5] Therefore, to speak of the "intended text" or derived text as a version is to speak of a nonextant form about which readers may legitimately disagree. Stillinger contends that

---

4. One notable exception is T. E. Lawrence's *The Mint,* published twenty years after the author's death, with word- and phrase-length blanks to expose the work of the censor.

5. Stillinger, "A Practical Theory of Versions," *Coleridge and Textual Instability: The Multiple Versions of the Major Poems* (Oxford University Press, 1994), 124–29.

is a good reason to reject the idealist/intentionalist view as an editorial goal. Donald Reiman calls such editing reader response criticism—a blatant form of interpretation, not scholarship.[6]

2. Other textual critics point out that in textual situations in which there are multiple variant documents, the variant forms can often be grouped into what look like attempts to reproduce accurately one version of the text.[7] Families, tribes, or clans of manuscripts are seen as various failed attempts to produce a not-yet-achieved ideal. So, if one attempt to reproduce a text accurately can fail, then each attempt, including the first one or the oldest one, could have failed. And, hence, every extant documentary text may be the result of a failure to represent "the text" accurately. The social-materialists admit this possibility, of course, but, by treating author and production crew as an authorizing team, they insist on the integrity of the extant product—a social artifact.

3. Furthermore, while it is true, as already stated, that readers attempting "to read through the physical document to the intended text" might occasionally disagree on what that intended text was or should be, it is also true that all one need do is to compose and print any such attempt and, voilà, there is now a physical document that can be considered a version of the work on an equal materialist footing (given the arguments in 1–3) with all other physical documents. But, the social-materialists might counter, though it is true that the new document has material existence and therefore an economic claim on our attention, we reserve the right to assess the authority by which each production process was undertaken. We choose to value the social contracts between the authors and their original publishers more highly than the (spurious?) authority you claim for subsequent editions. The authority for those later productions is of historical interest as part of cultural history (and perhaps as part of the history of editorial practice), but works of literary art *became* as the forces that made them possible worked together to produce the public work—leaving it stamped linguistically and bibliographically with the marks of that cooperative historical effort and event. Randall McLeod develops this view more coherently, persuasively, and rigidly than

---

6. Reiman, *Study of Modern Manuscripts,* 106–07.

7. See, for example, the *Donne Variorum* edition (University of Indiana Press) and the *Piers Plowman* electronic archive, in progress (University of Virginia).

any other writer, though in his own way Hans Zeller is also a radical proponent of this view of versions.[8]

A quite different take on the controversy of versions has developed in the last forty years among German editorial theorists, but their work has yet to have much impact on British and American thought. Obviously, the work of Hans Walter Gabler on James Joyce's texts has stimulated debate, but I for one saw his innovations regarding editorial procedure, particularly regarding the presentation of textual history and editorial emendations, as variations arising from Bowers's intentionalist views and copy-text editing. The recent publication of a collection of essays by German editors and theoreticians has helped to put Gabler's activities into a different context.[9]

I cannot here summarize with any subtlety, the growth and variations within the German school, but the idea of documentary integrity and the equation of versions with historical documents is sufficiently evident to strike a chord of sympathy among documentary, bibliographic, and sociologic editors as I have outlined them in this book. But the German editors seem keenly fixed also on authorial intentions. The notion of tracing authorial composition through genetic reconstructions emphasizing process and of finding in each historical document a locus for authorial meaning might seem alien to the orientations that respond favorably to the documentary emphasis. Thus, however, Anglo editors who emphasized authorial concerns will find much to empathize with in the German concern with authorial forms. It might appear to some that the German approach, particularly as outlined in Gabler's very helpful survey introducing the collection of German essays, but also in the individual essays as well, is bent on correcting the flawed emphases of all the Anglo orientations, suggesting a synthesis that should govern the editing of all texts. It remains to be seen how much influence this potent influx of Teutonic thought will wield in Anglo editorial circles.

There is no doubt that the questions of textual criticism are complex and that their application to the whole range of editorial problems is problematical. There is also no doubt that individual editors can and have botched their work in a large variety of ways. But these are not reasons to throw up one's hands and quit or retreat coweringly to the least

8. Randall McLeod, "Information on Information," *Text* 5 (1991): 241–81; Hans Zeller, "A New Approach to the Critical Constitution of Literary Texts," *Studies in Bibliography* 28 (1975): 231–64.

9. Hans Walter Gabler, George Bornstein, and Gillian Borland Pierce, editors, *Contemporary German Editorial Theory* (Ann Arbor: University of Michigan Press, 1995).

intrusive editorial stance. I return to a principle stated at the outset: that different questions about authors and their works can be answered better with a variety of tools than with just one. Works about which many people continue to ask questions need to be edited as archives of extant documents, annotated and introduced, *and* they need to be edited to extract the author's voice or at least to identify the variety of authorizing voices in the extant documents. As long as the proponents of the documentary, bibliographical, or sociological schools disparage the work of Bowers and his followers and apologize for their own contributions to that mode, and as long as intentionalist editors denigrate the work of these schools as timid at best and corruptive of authorial voices at worst—as long as editors continue to defend their own editorial goals by putting down alternative goals, general readers will continue to misunderstand the goals of editing and the usefulness of scholarly editions.

Part 2. Practice

Chapter Nine

Practical Effects

A range of textual situations can be cited to illustrate the practical effects of my arguments on specific problems in criticism. The effect most easily demonstrated is that produced by a work with two versions that our critical faculties lead us to see as meaning different things. It has been argued that a thoroughly revised work is a new work, not a new version of the same work. This argument is not one of substance but of terminology. It really does not matter if someone wants to call the manuscript of *The Red Badge* and the Appleton *The Red Badge* two different works, though it seems a waste of a good word, since the proportion of the two that is identical far exceeds that which is different. They are not different works in the same sense that *Maggie* and *The Red Badge* are. The important point is that the two are different and yet related. One's experience of each is informed and modified by knowledge of the other in ways far more intricate than is the case when one reads "genuinely" separate works by the same author.

Stephen Crane's canon offers several examples of works with significantly different versions about which editors and critics are in sharp disagreement. In 1894–95 Crane peddled *The Red Badge of Courage* around to several publishers, who would not touch it. Finally, after a weary year of rejections, and a successful excerpt in a newspaper, Crane accepted Appleton and Company's offer to publish it. There is some controversy over whether delays in publication were caused by proofreading problems or by difficulties Crane had in accepting the publisher's condition that certain changes be made. The changes, made by Crane himself in the extant manuscript, included some bowdlerization, but there is at least one change of paramount importance. According to Henry Binder and Hershel Parker, the original manuscript version has Henry Fleming merely exchange one version of romantic heroism for another equally conventional and unrealistic kind of heroism. This simple "no-win" exchange is obscured in the published text—the one that made Crane famous—because Fleming appears to adopt a more subtle or sophisticated view of courage. According to Fredson Bowers, editor of the Virginia edition of *The Red Badge,* Crane made all the manuscript changes before anyone at Appleton ever saw the work, submitting a typescript that already incorporated the revisions Parker and Binder think were imposed by the publisher. Further, Bowers claims that the differences in portraying Fleming's heroism between the original manuscript and the published work have been exaggerated. He, therefore, "established" an "eclectic text" that preserves, more or less, the final "artistic intentions" of the 1896 printed text.[1] A new text for the first time "restoring the manuscript" became available in 1979 in the *Norton Anthology of American Literature*.[2] Each edition claims to establish the text of *The Red Badge* as Crane wanted it. In short, each purports to be the real *Red Badge of Courage*. Since each is based on the same bibliographical evidence, it seems clear that critical interpretation of the evidence was crucial to the final state of the text in each case. It is possible, of course, that one or the other or both are inept executions of a critical point of view. Any editorial job, regardless of orientation, can be done well or poorly. The fundamental difference here is between two ways of constructing Stephen Crane from which two notions of his text are derived.[3]

Texts are used in different ways by different people. Anyone believing that Crane was pressured by the publisher to make the changes and therefore wishing to read and appreciate Crane's work as it stood in the original manuscript, uninfluenced by the radical effects publication had on the text, will find the Virginia edition very difficult to use. Anyone believing that Crane's manuscript revisions represent his attempts to work through the material toward his own notion of a finished and publishable work or anyone willing to say that works of art are products of authors and the influences on them—even that of publishers—will find the Norton

1. Edited by Fredson Bowers (Charlottesville: University of Virginia Press, 1975). Copy-text was the manuscript, of course, but most of the revisions of the Appleton edition were accepted as part of the final established text. See Bowers's arguments against Binder's view in "Authorial Intention and Editorial Problems," *Text* 5 (1991): 51–53.

2. Edited by Henry Binder for *The Norton Anthology of American Literature* (New York: W.W. Norton, 1979), 2:802–906.

3. See James L. W. West, "Editing as Biography," *Studies in the Novel* 27 (1995); 295–303, for an interesting elaboration of this idea.

text somehow incomplete. Likewise, students of cultural history, given the manuscript version newly edited for the *Norton Anthology* and told it was the text of *The Red Badge*, would be at sixes and sevens to explain the criticism, popular appreciation, and literary allusion in studies based on the Appleton text. And yet, until the Norton text appeared, all readers had been misled by published editions, including the Virginia edition, about Crane's original conception of heroism for Fleming.[4] Whether or not one considers the Virginia edition or the Norton "well-edited texts," both the early version and the published version are of primary importance; neither is the whole text of *The Red Badge*. They are separate authorial versions, representing more or less well what Crane intended at two different times under two different sets of circumstances.[5]

It is sometimes argued that to intend cetain meanings or words for a work is different from intending to do whatever is necessary in order to get those words published. Such arguments are used to justify texts incorporating the "artistic" revisions but rejecting the "imposed" revisions of later versions. I would not say that the procedure is illegitimate, only that it tends to violate the historical integrity of versions, represents an attempt to create a single best text, and tends to confuse the record of the variant documents of the work of art. The critic approaching one version with full cognizance of the other is in a better position to understand each than is the critic seeing only one, even when that one is a melding of the two—or more.

Hershel Parker's discussion of Norman Mailer's *An American Dream* provides a complication. Parker concludes that Mailer's initial intentions were subverted significantly in mid-composition by the assassination of John F. Kennedy, who was a character in the book. According to Parker, the revision in the Dial publication suffers from inadequate control by Mailer over all the consequences of revision.[6] Parker argues for the superiority

---

4. Bowers objected to this statement ("Authorial Intention," 53), either because it accepts the notion that the early and late versions of the work *are* radically different (he thought not) or because it suggests that the late version is not really Crane's (he thought so). But, regardless of who is right, it took the Norton edition to bring the early manuscript version to the public in a readable form.

5. Bowers also objected to this statement, contending that the early manuscript version represents a draft and was never intended in a public sense by Crane. Hershel Parker's extended commentary on these two editions (*Flawed Texts and Verbal Icons* (Chicago: Northwestern University Press, 1984): 147–79) provides many more details and a very different conclusion, which seems to suggest that only one is the real text—Binder's.

6. Hershel Parker, "Norman Mailer's Revisions of the *Esquire* Version of *An American Dream* and the Aesthetic Problem of 'Built-in Unintentionality'" *Bulletin of Research in the Humanities* 84 (Winter 1981): 405–30, passim; *Flawed Texts and Verbal Icons*, chap. 7.

of the initial (*Esquire*) version on the grounds that it is a more coherent piece of art than is the revision, and he wants Mailer to restore and improve the earlier version. Parker is much more concerned with showing how the revision destroys the original coherence than he is in sounding out the potential coherence of the revision. One might with equal justice want Mailer to fulfill the potential of his revised version by improving it. If Mailer did either of these things, we would have, of course, a third version. Our understanding of each would be influenced and, I dare say, enriched by knowledge of the other two because the work of art is the imagined whole implied by the differing authoritative forms. In a real sense the work is in the reader's experience of it, and his apprehension of it is significantly enhanced by exposure to the work in its variant authoritative forms.

The effect on criticism of recognizing multiple versions can also be shown in works existing in two versions that do not differ substantially in overall meaning, resulting from revisions that might be judged by some to be "horizontal."[7] Thackeray's *Pendennis* was written in 1847–49 for serial publication and revised sometime in 1853–54 for a "cheap" edition, which was published in October 1855 (dated 1856).[8] As far as social satire is concerned, *Pendennis* began where *Vanity Fair* left off. It has been argued, however, that Thackeray mellowed after his nearly fatal illness in the autumn of 1848, which interrupted the composition and serialization of *Pendennis* halfway through, though the Horatian mood of an older, more secure, established author is more noticeable in *Esmond* (1852) and *The Newcomes* (1854–55) than in the second half of *Pendennis*. The revisions for the cheap edition of *Pendennis* made in 1854 quite clearly reflect that mellowing.[9] Certain revisions were merely mechanical. For example, the revised edition was unillustrated, and so all references to illustrations were removed from the text. Moreover, since the new edition was the "cheap edition," nothing was added to the text; instead, the equivalent of eighteen pages was cut. In choosing what to cut, an author can of course make more than mechanical choices. Among the passages to go were a very few that were merely repetitious, but the major cuts had the effect of toning down

7. The term is Tanselle's for revisions that enhance a previously articulated intention—as opposed to "vertical" revisions, which alter the basic intentions and result in a "new work" or at least new version (Tanselle, "Editorial Problem of Final Authorial Intention," 1976; rpt. in *Selected Studies in Bibliography* (Charlottesville: U P of Virginia, 1979), 334–35.

8. W. M. Thackeray, *The History of Pendennis*, 2 vols. (London: Bradbury and Evans, 1849–50); reprinted in a "cheap," one-volume rev. ed. (London: Bradbury and Evans, 1856).

9. A fuller discussion of the changes appears in Peter Shillingsburg, "Thackeray's *Pendennis* Revised," *Etudes Anglaises* 34 (1981): 432–42.

satiric remarks: Helen Pendennis no longer suffers "under such an infernal tyranny as only women can inflict on, or bear from, one another," and Pen's friend Foker is no longer described as a "stupid ass." Some remarks about village gossip and one fairly long digression on lovemaking were removed. In the process of toning things down and shortening the book, however, Thackeray also touched up some passages in ways that show a master stylist at work. And, particularly near the beginning of the book, Thackeray also eliminated some character descriptions that, in the light of later developments in this serialized novel, seem like false starts. On the whole, though, reduction in length and a response to the critics' charges of misanthropy governed the alterations. One need not expect more, since Thackeray's continuing writing commitments as well as the commercial purposes of the cheap edition probably prevented him from major rewriting or additions. We have, then, two versions of *Pendennis,* each representing slightly different literary values; readers should be able to study texts of both. They need not think of one or the other as the best text, though each person may have his own preference.

Even where no positively authorial text survives, our view of the work is complex. I would like to show not only how the arguments of this essay affect our view of Keats's "Ode on a Grecian Urn" but also how they would lead to a presentation of the materials different from that used in the most carefully produced scholarly edition of the poem, in Jack Stillinger's *The Poems of John Keats*.[10]

The original manuscript for the poem is lost. Charles Brown made a copy from Keats's manuscript, and three other men made transcripts of Brown's copy. Brown's copy was apparently the source text for the first publication in *Annals of the Fine Arts* (1820), though another copy may have intervened or another authorial copy may have been the source. The *Annals* text was probably the basis for the poem's reprinting in *Lamia, Isabella, The Eve of St. Agnes, and Other Poems* (1820).

The variants in the manuscript transcripts are restricted to punctuation, capitalization, hyphenation, and the substitution of *will* for *can* in line 40 ("and not a soul to tell / Why thou art desolate, can [*or* will] e'er return.") Although the substitution makes perfectly good sense and does not affect the rhythm, the "established" text has a note calling the change a "copying error."[11] The reason is not clear, but it is likely that Stillinger felt

---

10. John Keats, *The Poems of John Keats* (Cambridge: Belknap Press of Harvard University Press, 1978), 372–73.
11. Keats, *Poems*, 653.

an obligation to justify his single established text. He cites no evidence to indicate that it was a copying error. I belabor this point because an editor's desire for a single established text (and probably the readers' and critics' similar desires) has seemed in the past to require the "rejection" of variant versions.

When the poem was published in *Annals of the Fine Arts* in January 1820, several variants crept in. They may or may not be authorial. The word *Ode* is left out of the title; a comma is added after *still* in line 1, making what had appeared to be a synonym for *yet* into what appears to be a synonym for *motionless*. According to the notes in Stillinger's edition, *Annals* introduced three variants by copy error: (1) in line 8 "What men or gods are these" became "What Gods or Men are these" (this could instead be a revision); (2) in line 16 "nor ever can those trees be bare" became "nor ever bid the spring adieu" (this really is an error—an inadvertent repetition of line 22); and (3) in line 22 "nor ever bid the spring adieu" became "nor never bid the spring adieu." One might guess that a printing house reader caught and corrected the "nor never" error in line 22 in proof and that the corrected line was misplaced in line 16—but that is mere speculation, and, in any case, I think it is easy to see that 2 and 3 are errors.

In addition *Annals* introduced two new readings deemed acceptable for Stillinger's edition: in line 34 "all her silken sides with garlands drest?" became "all her silken flanks with garlands drest?"; and in line 47 "Thou wilt remain . . . as friend" became "Thou wilt remain . . . a friend"—either change, for all anyone can prove, could be copying errors. Note two things: first, the only change introduced in the *Annals* text that seems to change meaning is the comma after *still*; the other changes only offer alternatives that tease one into guessing what the improvement is or what sort of verbal sensitivity triggered the changes. Second, in the Stillinger edition the comma after *still* is recorded in a textual footnote but not in the textual notes at the back of the book. But the only way to find out that the variants in lines 34 and 48 were also introduced in the *Annals* text is to go to the textual notes at the end of the book. Presenting an orderly history of the changes was not of primary importance in this edition.

When the poem was reprinted in *Lamia, Isabella, The Eve of St. Agnes, and Other Poems*, the text restored *Ode* to the title and removed the comma after *still* and corrected the three *Annals* errors by restoring the readings in Brown's manuscript. In addition, in line 9 "What love? what dance?" became "What mad pursuit?"; in line 18 the bold lover "Though winning near the goal" was told "O, do not grieve" but this became "yet, do not grieve"; and in line 47 "Thou wilt remain, in midst of other woe/Than ours" became "Thou shalt remain, in midst of other woe/Than ours." And, finally, the 1820 book text is the only one to add the famous quotation marks in line 49.

In a sense we have no authorial text at all, since Keats's own manuscript has disappeared and the printed texts are based, so far as we know, on Brown's transcript or a copy made from it. Yet it can be argued that there are three versions; for, even though we have no external evidence to say Keats was responsible for any of the variants, it is not unlikely that he was. A textual critic using the tools of his trade intelligently can identify and eliminate obvious scribal errors, and he could easily report the alternative remaining readings in historical progression (unlike the form in Stillinger's edition). If the editor did, each reader could easily use the available evidence himself to see the successive viable forms of the work. If a work is the imagined whole implied by the range of variant authorial versions, then a single best text of the "Ode" is inadequate. It is interesting that in the array of textual variation in "Ode on a Grecian Urn" the most significant alternate readings are "accidentals"—the comma after *still* and the quotation marks in line 49. I think we should be content with the ambiguities supplied and should reject attempts to establish a single best text. We have, in fact, three slightly variant versions, each dating from a distinct moment in the preparation of texts of the poem. And the variants (other than the errors) draw attention to nuances of meaning that might otherwise receive less notice.

One last example, the controversy over Hans Walter Gabler's synoptic and critical edition of James Joyce's *Ulysses,* will illustrate the profound difference made by incompatible understandings of what constitutes the work and by opposing orientations toward the work in conceiving proper editorial vehicles for texts.[12]

---

12. The controversy is very well developed, and I list only a few of the most well-known items: John Kidd, "The Scandal of *Ulysses,*" *New York Review of Books,* 30 June 1988, 32–39; "An Inquiry into *Ulysses: The Corrected Text,*" *PBSA* 82 (1988): 411–584. Hans Walter Gabler, "Synchrony and Diachrony of Texts: Practice and Theory of the Critical Edition of James Joyce's *Ulysses,*" *Text* 1 (1984): 305–26; "The Text as Process and Problem of Intentionality," *Text* 3 (1987): 107–16; "Textual Studies and Criticism," *Library Chronicle of the University of Texas at Austin* 20 (1990): 151–65; "Unsought Encounters," in *Devils and Angels,* ed. Philip Cohen (University Press of Virginia, 1991), 152–66; "On Textual Criticism and Editing: The Case of Joyce's *Ulysses,*" in *Palimpsest: Editorial Theory in the Humanities,* ed. George Bornstein and Ralph G. Williams (University of Michigan Press, 1993), 195–224; and, his most specific response to Kidd, "What 'Ulysses' Requires," *PBSA* 87 (1993): 187–248. Among the best-known and substantive commentaries by others: Michael Gro-

A good deal has been made about errors and their correction in this controversy, and both sides have accused the other of labeling bad judgment as error. Suffice here to say that both sides have made errors and that, from my point of view, it appears that the label "bad judgment" tends to eminate from one orientation toward texts about the acts of editors operating within a different orientation toward texts. Nevertheless, it is the debatable matters that draw my attention the most. I believe an explanation for the controversy can be found in an attempt to identify points of view and assumptions behind the differences of opinion about the state of Joyce's text. These differences fall into categories, which I would like to present as a series of oppositions between Gabler and Kidd, which I think account for the surface differences between them about debatable matters—such as how an edition of *Ulysses* should be prepared.[13]

Gabler's edition of Joyce makes certain things about his procedure very clear. One of them is that he thinks the manuscript and typescript materials, taken together, form a sound foundation for identifying and correcting errors of omission and commission in the 1922 edition of *Ulysses*. His position on this is so strongly presented in his edition that there is never a moment when it seemed likely that anything other than the manuscripts taken together should be the starting point for a new edition.

Kidd is equally clear in his preference for the 1922 edition as the starting point for a new edition. He cites Gaskell's essay in *Writer to Reader* and McGann's review of Gabler's edition as corroborating spirits (nay, he cites them as if they were authorities) favoring the 1922 edition as a copytext. One might argue that there is enough evidentiary material surviving to edit this work from either direction and produce approximately the same

den, "Foostering over Those Changes: The New *Ulysses*," *James Joyce Quarterly* 22 (1984): 137–59; Jerome McGann, *"Ulysses* as a Postmodern Text: The Gabler Edition," *Criticism* 27 (1985): 283–306; Groden, "A Response to John Kidd's 'An Inquiry Into *Ulysses: The Corrected Text*,'" *James Joyce Quarterly* 28 (1990): 81–110; and Kidd's article "Gabler's Errors in Context: A Reply to Michael Groden on Editing *Ulysses*," *James Joyce Quarterly* 28 (1990): 111–51; David Greetham, "The Manifestation and Accommodation of Theory in Textual Editing," in *Devils and Angels*, 78–102; and Vicki Mahaffey, "Intentional Error: The Paradox of Editing Joyce's *Ulysses*," in *Representing Modernist Texts: Editing as Interpretation*, ed. George Bornstein (University of Michigan Press, 1991), 171–91.

13. Michael Groden, citing the notion of irreconcilable editorial orientations from a previous edition of this book, articulated this argument as a minor part of his "Response to John Kidd's 'An Inquiry'" (92); and Kidd refers genially to the same book in his response to Groden ("Gabler's Errors," 122, 125). But Kidd's remark that, "according to Mr. Shillingburg's scheme, all [orientations] direct attention to context, and all require precise registration and handling of variants," suggests to me that he does not agree that the different orientations justify both different assessments of evidence and different uses of it.

text; so, in itself this difference does not explain why Kidd is so opposed to Gabler's edition or why Gabler does not accede immediately to Kidd's arguments.

A second item of contention is also very clearly expressed by Gabler. While acknowledging that Joyce was an innovative and sometimes deliberately obscure writer, he favors the view that Joyce was sometimes an inattentive and careless scribe or proofreader of his own work. This possibility is so clearly before him that Gabler seems to read revisions and scribal copies (whether in Joyce's hand or not) very suspiciously. He thinks, for example, that when Joyce changed "A lonely last candle" by crossing out *lonely* and interlining *long* ambiguously after *last*, he really meant to interline *lonely*; he thinks, further, that, in copying his draft into the Rosenbach manuscript, Joyce misread his own handwriting, producing "A last long candle" and writing the word *last* ambiguously so that a typist misread it as *lost*, producing the final misreading, "A lost long candle," in 1922. Gabler emends to "A last lonely candle", restoring, he feels, authorial intention over scribal inattention.[14] One might add that his emended reading has the virtue of making sense.

On the other hand, Kidd favors the view that Joyce's hand is to be trusted whenever possible. While acknowledging that any copyist, even an author, will make mistakes, Kidd seems to want to assume, wherever possible, that Joyce deliberately made most of the changes, even the revisions and deletions that show up in a typescript or proof or published work without holograph support. He tends to read the progressive record sympathetically. For example, he believes that when Joyce crossed out *lonely* and interlined *long*, he meant it. He does not find the Rosenbach manuscript inscription of the word *lost* at all ambiguous. So, when the passage became "A lost long candle" in the Rosenbach manuscript, Kidd assumes Joyce meant that, too.[15] He does not say whether "A lost long candle" is comprehensible. In fact, it seems significant that neither man in discussing this passage comments on its meaning.

A third matter is not so clearly expressed by either man, but I think I've figured it out with the help of Gabler's 1991 explanations in "On Textual Criticism and Editing" in *Palimpsest*. Gabler dispensed with traditional tabulations of manuscript alterations, emendations, and historical collations; instead, he developed a new method of reporting the genetic development

---

14. *Ulysses*, 2:814, 3:1744; Rosenbach,*Ulysses: A Facsimile of the Manuscript,* (New York: Octagon Books, 1975), vol. 2, episode 13, fol. 55.

15. Kidd, "An Inquiry," 432.

of composition into which he folded the report of his own editorial decisions. Although he provides, at the end of volume 3 of his edition, a fairly detailed description of the specific manuscripts and typescripts that preceded the first edition, he does not, in the continuous manuscript text or its footnotes, identify the precise document in which each reading occurred. Instead, he constructs an account of the process of inscription and revision, indicating the type of document and its existence or nonexistence. In effect, Gabler used each extant document as a copy-text from which to construct the continuous manuscript text by interpreting the information about revision from them. He did this by transcribing each document into the netted array of the manuscript and typescript material, called the continuous manuscript text. This new networked transcription is itself an edited text, which is then used as the copy-text for the clear reading text. It does not take a rocket scientist to figure out that, if an error is made in an edited text, which is then used as the basis for a further text, the final product will be at least as flawed as its intermediate text. This difficulty, this possibility for the proliferation of error, is one Gabler fully understood and accepted as a risk undertaken in his attempt to work forward through the composition process toward the intended publication, which in 1922 resulted in so many errors.

On the other hand, Kidd favors a traditional apparatus in which there is only one step from the copy-text to the finally edited text. A historical collation and a list of emendations would avoid the risk of compounded error. If errors were made, they would each be made only once; their correction would then be a matter of verification. There being no manuscript form of the work that represented any one stage in the composition for the whole novel, this demand for a single complete copy-text and list of emendations is rather difficult to meet if the copy-text is a manuscript. But from Kidd's point of view that is not a problem, since the 1922 edition does represent (to him) such a stage and is his preferred choice as copy-text. Kidd's position on this matter is reflected clearly in his attitude toward the authority of later texts when changes of unknown origin appear: the later text has, he says, "presumptive authority" over the earlier version (426), even when the early text is Joyce's manuscript and the later text is scribal.

Given these fundamental differences between the two men about how an edition should be constructed and presented, it is no wonder that the work of one is unsatisfactory to the other. Given the magnitude of the task, it will be a red-letter day when an editor of *Ulysses* produces an edition that not only completely fulfills his stated goals but does so without any errors of commission or omission.

But these considerations do not account for the animus in the controversy. Nor do I think there is any justification for a rhetoric of certainty when it is applied to matters open for debate. Real debate is not acrimonious—it may be blunt—but its purpose is to lead to a fuller understanding of the enterprise to which we are jointly committed. One final point of contention illustrates, I think, the fact that fundamental differences about the goals of an edition and the proper emendation procedures lead to misunderstandings that appear more important than they really are.

At the end of a half-page discussion of the development of the phrase in which James Stephen (the revolutionary) is compared to Garibaldi (the "Irish Garibaldi"), Kidd seems surprised that Gabler's edition and the 1922 edition end with the same reading.[16] Kidd's beef here is not with the reading text but with two other matters: first, that Gabler's editorial decision here does not follow the same pattern found in the example of the "last lonely candle" and, second, that the record in the synoptic and critical edition is misleading about the facts. The first issue seems to me an indication that Kidd has not fully assimilated or understood Gabler's editorial procedure. I cannot tell whether this is because Kidd could not follow Gabler's explanation or because his assumptions about proper editorial procedures blind him to the rationality of a procedure built on a different notion of texts. The second issue, I think, illustrates the way a predisposition to find fault obscures what was actually being reported. Gabler reports the deletion of *Irish* as a level-B deletion by Joyce in a document now lost.[17] Kidd emphasizes that the deletion could have been a scribal oversight or just about anything, since whatever happened to the word *Irish* happened offstage, so to speak. He is right, of course, but he expected Gabler to prefer the extant manuscript reading over the lost, possibly scribal reading. He seems not to be able to understand how Gabler could reject *lost long candle* because it was possibly scribal but accept the deletion of *Irish* despite is status as possibly scribal. And why, without knowing for sure, does Gabler report it as Joyce's change? A sympathetic reading of the synoptic and critical edition would conclude, I think, that Gabler has admitted that the deletion was made offstage *and* that he conjectures Joyce made the deletion. To an unsympathetic reader it may look as though Gabler has claimed as fact something that is debatable; to the sympathetic eye it appears that Gabler has made an editorial decision, reported it, and assumed that any

16. "An Inquiry," 450.
17. *Ulysses*, 1:344–45.

reader would know that it was an editorial decision, because the evidence is no longer extant.

There never was and never will be an edition that is not put in a certain light—that does not ask readers to understand the author to be a certain kind of author and to take the book to be a certain kind of book. Too much of what we do is debatable for it to be any other way. When Kidd's edition appears, it too will put the text and its author in a certain light. Then we shall see what practical differences are made by editing *Ulysses* as Gabler has done and as Kidd would have it done. We will see how readings are affected by principles leading to different choices. Will certain scenes face each other across a deliberate gutter margin in one and not the other? Will certain scenes be deleted? Will sentences read one way and not another? And what will the reader be told about passages that appear only in an apparatus and not as part of the "established, standard, scholarly, definitive, critical edition"? We do not need the rhetoric of definitive, final, standard, established, be-all and end-all scholarly editions. There never was one and never will be.

We look at the history of editions, and, in Gabler's words, "we may see theoretical assumptions of the editorial goal for textual criticism superseding one another as in a palimpsest, each taking recourse to copy-text as an expedient of procedural methodology."[18] The only word I disagree with there is *superseding*—each new scholarly edition, unless carelessly produced, extends the shelf on which there is still space.

---

18. Gabler, "On Textual Criticism and Editing," 205.

Chapter Ten

Copy-Texts and Apparatuses

The thrust of this book has been fourfold: first, to explore the complexity of what a work of literary art is and the relationship between the work and the variant texts of the work; second, to establish that reading a single text of a work of art as if it adequately represented the work or were in fact the work may limit the reader's access to the whole work of art; third, to understand the different approaches to texts and the different needs represented by editors and critics who disagree over how a particular work should be edited; and, fourth, to suggest both the legitimacy and the essential irreconcilability of five different approaches to editing works of literary art.

This is not to say that all editorial theories are equally good or that careful attention to theory is no longer needed. On the contrary, the editorial responsibility is now greater than it has ever been. Readers are no longer content for an editor to say that his choice of copy-text follows the standard Greg rationale or that the emendations include silent regularization of accidentals or that copy-text has been chosen on the basis of the author's final intentions or on the publisher's and author's best collaboration. Editors can no longer act as if the standards of scholarly editing have now in the last decade of the twentieth century reached a plateau of excellence and universal applicability. Nor can the reviewer any longer say of a new edition that it either follows or violates standard scholarly editorial procedures. Both editor and reader must be prepared to identify which version of a work or what orientation toward the formal elements of a work is being employed to prepare the clear-reading text, distinguishing that text from the other potential texts that lie within the array of texts representing the work. Both editor and reader must be able to say how the clear reading text of the work represents the work and how the alternate versions are represented within the scholarly edition. Responsible criticism, based on awareness of the context of utterance (biographical, cultural, linguistic, political, historical, and so forth), cannot be blind to the important evidence of context found in variant authorial versions and publication history (including author-publisher relations and histories of book production).

Trivial examples illustrate this principle better than situations of substance because we are not distracted by meaning. Samuel Clemens, on his tour of Australia, told his Adelaide audiences, as he may have told others, that the character Smiley in his celebrated story of the jumping frog was originally named Greeley. But the poverty-stricken magazine in which it first appeared "had not enough 'G's' and so they changed Greeley's name to 'Smiley.' That's a fact."[1] Actually, that was not a fact, since the story had appeared already in a California paper with the name Smiley. But Twain was not complaining; he must have enjoyed telling about it and no doubt would take a whimsical view of any editorial effort to restore the original. Twain's anecdote provides us with a partial record of composition, giving us an alternative that modifies the text most widely known. It would be pointless to argue over which was the "right" text. They are both right in their own way, even though, according to the story, Twain is not the author of the name Smiley.

The needs that bring editors to the task of producing a new edition of a work are personal needs. The editor's formal orientation, whatever its basic configuration and however much qualified, is also a personal one. The editor, for his own sake, must fulfill his needs, following his formal orientations with integrity and logic. When he provides an edition for the scholarly community at large, however, he incurs a responsibility to provide for scholars whose formal orientations differ from his own. While in most cases editors cannot and will not provide four clear texts of a work, they can and must do two things: (1) make clear which text they have provided, and (2) provide a usable apparatus with enough information to satisfy users who disagree legitimately with the editorial principles. A third requirement may be self-evident: that the new edition text be presented as "a text among several potential texts" rather than as "the standard text," reliable and complete in itself. As I noted before, the intensity of Donald Pizer's antagonism for James West's edition of *Sister Carrie* seems to have been triggered mostly by the idea that the editors offered this early text as a "replacement" for the traditional text. After attempting to lay to

---

1. *South Australia Register*, 14 Oct. 1895.

rest the notion that West's text was "the" *Sister Carrie,* Pizer concludes by expressing gratitude for the existence of this "original version."[2]

Enough has been written by Greg, Tanselle, and Bowers to explain, from within the authorial orientation, the basic principles for choosing copy-text. McGann and Gaskell have written cogently from the sociological orientation on behalf of printed texts as copy-texts. Both arguments posit general rules upon which to rely when conclusive evidence is unavailable to guide the editor. Greg assumed that publishers tend to mar authorial forms; followers of Greg rely on manuscripts or texts "close to the manuscript" because they see printed texts that are actually better representations of the author's work as exceptions to the rule. They therefore demand proof of the superiority of printed texts before adopting them as copy-texts. McGann, on the other hand, assumes that modern publishers tend to take better care of accidentals than authors do. Followers of the sociological school see the printed product in modern times as a naturally superior, more presentable form of the work and require proof that a manuscript is a better representation of the work before reverting to it as copy-text. McGann finds a rare example in Shelley's manuscripts.[3] In short, both arguments allow for exceptions and require that evidence running contrary to the general rule be provided in order to countermand that rule.

Editors have been following these various orientations for years. Reviewers praise or damn new editions not only for being accurate or inaccurate, not only for recovering or not recovering all the relevant foundation material for a new edition, but also for following or not following a particular orientation. The amazing thing has been the single-mindedness of each school in thinking theirs is the higher course, though standards of polite behavior require that genteel methods be employed in describing the inferiority of the opposition's editions and of the logic that produced them. It would help matters for editors to acknowledge not the correctness but the legitimacy of opposing viewpoints: to explore the felt needs that the different approaches seek to fulfill and to create editions that at least acknowledge the potential of other approaches.

Fredson Bowers's remark in the Ohio State University Press Hawthorne edition that, editorially speaking, the cards were on the table face up in the textual introduction and apparatus tables was hailed for its no-

---

2. Review in *American Literature* 53 (1981): 737.
3. McGann, *Critique of Modern Textual Criticism* (Chicago: University of Chicago Press, 1983), 108.

ble intent, before two serious shortcomings became apparent.[4] First, as edition users we suddenly realized that the cards were not all there: accidentals were omitted from the historical collation because of expense. Editors consoled us subsequently by inventing a category of "semisubstantives" for accidentals that affected meaning, and we considered the loss of the rest (accidentals that did not affect meaning) a welcome relief from triviality. A few scholars carped at this compromise because of what it did to the definitions of accidentals and substantives, but on the whole it seemed better than the alternative (print everything), and it saved the best part of what was meant by laying the cards on the table face up. The reader could see what the editor had done and most of the material he had worked from.

But a second flaw soon appeared. Readers discovered that they were not interested in what the editor had done. Editors were uninteresting, and the apparatus—designed to show what the editor had done—was designed to show the wrong thing. Emendations lists showed the changes made by the editor: some because the author had made them; some because a previous editor had made a seemingly necessary correction; some because the present editor thought they were necessary (all these in a single undifferentiated list). The historical collation showed other forms the text had taken that the present editor did not adopt: some because the author did not make them; some because, though made by the author, they were made for the wrong reasons or under duress or other mitigating circumstance. Again, a single undifferentiated list was provided. Readers, meanwhile, vacillated between wanting, on the one hand, to know the variant versions of the work—the development of meaningful textual forms—and, on the other hand, to forget the whole thing as more trouble than the effort of deciphering and sifting an apparatus was worth.

To add to the problem, during this time publication budgets were shrinking, and apparatus costs were rising. If the report on accidentals in the historical collation could be curtailed, editors reasoned, perhaps other lists could be pruned, too. Whenever an apparatus is shortened or dispensed with altogether, as is often the case with classroom texts, it is a clear indication that scholarly editions are thought to provide the correct text, adequate for study. Alternate versions of the work were surely not highly prized by editors, who began eliminating what they called "pre-copy-text" forms.[5] Their arguments went something like this: not only are alterations

---

4. Intro. to Nathaniel Hawthorne, *The Scarlet Letter* (Columbus: Ohio State University Press, 1962), xlvii.

5. The Cambridge D. H. Lawrence and Indiana C. S. Peirce editions are prime examples, though by no means the only ones.

in manuscripts difficult to sort out, but their presentation in printed form is inexact and expensive. So, why not say that scholars interested in the arcane, pre-copy-text forms must go to the original manuscripts? Accordingly, one important aspect of "the work" was jettisoned from many scholarly editions, the primary justification lying in the pejorative connotations of the word *arcane*.

Objecting mildly to the apparatus of the State University of New York Press edition of Cooper's *Pioneers* in a review, Hershel Parker points out that the editor lists "rejected readings" from unimportant printed editions but does not report the authorial revisions from the manuscript. He wondered, as we all should, why this should be the case.[6] I do not agree with Parker that no harm results from such listings; undifferentiated tables of variants, clotted with insignificant and nonauthorial material, confirm critics in the habit of not using the apparatuses of critical editions because they cannot imagine what to use them for. A scholarly edition, in order to be worthy of the name, must not only present a clear text representing a logically conceived form of the work but also provide an apparatus revealing the development of the work—its various versions, authorial and collaborative— so that students can include in their exploration of the work's context the trial, alternative, and "externally influenced" utterances that were or remain a part of the work.

Editors who do this well will not be as anxious to lay the cards of their own work on the table face up as they will be to lay the identifiable work of the author and his or her collaborators there. Tables of variants will be redesigned to show, when it can be determined, who introduced each variant, when it was introduced, and under what circumstances. If revealing the development and alteration of the work is the primary purpose of the apparatus, then it will be looked upon as a resource, not as a collection of rejected and superseded scraps from the workshop floor—curiosities of passing interest. As the examples from the Thackeray material presented in earlier chapters well show, things that at first seem trivial can in fact be very significant. Editors will be presenting significant information about the work of art, not just listing required textual histories. Perhaps the least useful purpose of the apparatus record is to provide a place to which, in a mildly paranoid way, one can look to see that the editor has not abused the power over the literary work.

Lest all this sound noble but impractical, I show in part 3 how computers make it all possible.

---

6. *Nineteenth Century Fiction* 33 (Sept. 1981): 201.

Part 3. Practicalities

Chapter Eleven

Economics and Editorial Goals

Money (whether scarce or abundant) and technology (in more ways every year) affect editorial goals and even editorial principles. The ebb and flow of financial support for editing ushers in and out the current fashions in editorial theory. In short, not only are there legitimate differences in editorial goals based on differences in formal orientations and other theoretical concepts, but there are also practical differences in editorial goals that are imposed by economic influences.

When the first edition of this book was being prepared, technology for scholarly editions included the printing press, two types of optical collating machines for comparison of multiple copies from the same edition, and the beginnings of computer use in word processing, indexing, concordances, and typesetting. In those days the computing systems used in commercial typesetting were incompatible with the computing systems used in most universities. Now desktop publishing with laser printers is nearly as common as typewriters and photocopying were fifteen years ago, and the printed book is no longer thought of as the best form in which to distribute scholarly editions. Hypertext, multimedia, virtual imaging, compact disks, and the Internet are the wave of the future. Coding transcripts and editions for typesetting barely got a foothold in the editorial workshop before universal coding systems for electronic distribution of texts and images became desirable.

My primary concern here is with the way in which money and technology affect editorial theory and practice. Practical guides to the use of specific software applications and hardware will have to be sought elsewhere. The specific references I make to programs and applications and machinery may already sound quaint by the time this book sees print. This chapter will focus primarily on financial considerations and traditional book publication, which remain important if fading concerns to scholarly editors. Electronic technology will occupy the remainder of the book.

It is useful in this regard to think of scholarly editing as having at least three ideals desirable separately or in tandem, depending on how much one can afford. The first is to rescue lost works from oblivion. Another is to rescue badly produced or reproduced works from textual corruption. A third, more ambitious ideal is to provide a rich resource for textual study of a work. Time and money are as important as intelligence and ambition in determining what the scholarly editor can do to fulfill these ideals.

The least the editor can do is to make available a "lost" work. That involves finding the work—which is usually lost because it only ever existed in a manuscript or a single obscure or ephemeral publication. Once found the work must be reproduced. Its condition determines how much must be done, but the scholarly editor is primarily a preserver, not a merchandiser, and his simplest objectives may be met with a photofacsimile reprint or an unedited transcription. The principles for editing single-text works are not what I want to explore here, but I would like to acknowledge that there are complex considerations involved, even though I think it is the simplest of editorial problems.

Let me give an example. William Gilmore Simms, a prolific South Carolina writer, produced in 1869, under desperate post–Civil War conditions, a novel called *The Cub of the Panther,* which was published in the cramped columns of a New York monthly magazine—too far removed for any authorial proofreading. The novel exists nowhere else. It is a lost work, produced badly, in a single ephemeral publication not susceptible to facsimile reproduction. The only surviving manuscript is of two chapters that somehow were omitted from the magazine. A mere rescue effort would require only that the editor supply a straight transcription of the magazine text. Higher ambitions and more time for research and money for travel would require the restoration of the manuscript chapters from the South Caroliniana Library in Columbia, South Carolina. Even higher ideals and more time and money would call for identification of source passages in Simms's unpublished 1847 journal of his travels to the area of North Carolina that furnished the novel's setting. An editor with time and money could add the attention necessary to remove, by judicious alteration, the apparent errors and, possibly, nonauthorial house styling in the printed text. And that is to say nothing about historical introductions and annotations.[1]

If the work to be edited exists in multiple texts, the problem is more complex. Research time must be devoted to ferreting out the compositional history or the textual history of the work to determine which texts bear authority. The editor may still, because of limited resources in time or money, choose simply to reproduce a historically significant or authoritative text without the added effort of producing a critical text or of providing the full scope of textual materials a critic might want. Classroom texts provide many examples—both good and bad—of this sort of editing. The Modern Library edition of George Meredith's *The Ordeal of Richard Feverel*, introduced by Lionel Stevenson, is reprinted from the first edition (1859) because, in Stevenson's opinion, the revisions made for subsequent editions were "so roughly handled as to suggest haste and impatience" and "wrought positive harm upon the story."[2] The Dover Publications edition of the same novel reprints a revised edition (Boston, 1888) that "incorporates further emendations by the author."[3] The Dover text gives no analysis of the nature or effects of the revisions, nor does it mention what else might have been incorporated in this late U.S. edition. Readers, of course, are at the mercy of the thoroughness and perspicuity of the editor's research in these matters, and conscientious searchers may be less fortunate in their choices of texts than more casual editors. In the first edition of this book I gave as an example of a poorly chosen text Sheridan Baker's edition of Henry Fielding's *Tom Jones*. I said:

> It was produced before Fredson Bowers and Martin Battestin's more ambitious scholarly edition. Baker determined by a line of reasoning Bowers confutes that the fourth edition of *Tom Jones* represented Fielding's final wishes and that it was perhaps the most carefully proofread of the five editions Fielding could have supervised. Relying on collations completed and reported over thirty years earlier only as a basis for his choice of copy-text, Baker "reprinted" the fourth edition, supplying in an appendix the one major third-edition revision that somehow was omitted from the fourth. This [I concluded with ill-based

---

1. Miriam Shillingsburg, "An Edition of William Gilmore Simms's *The Cub of the Panther*," dissertation, University of South Carolina, 1969.

2. Lionel Stevenson, intro. to George Meredith, *The Ordeal of Richard Feverel* (New York: Random House, 1950), xxv.

3. Copyright notice in George Meredith, *The Ordeal of Richard Feverel* (New York: Dover Publications, 1983).

confidence] is not critical editing; it rescues a text of some historical interest, but restores nothing.

Well, it is true that Baker's edition is not more than a reprint of a single historical text—but his choice was much better than I was led to believe by Bowers's Wesleyan edition of *Tom Jones*. Bowers's argument was based on a misinterpretation of the bibliographical evidence concerning the third edition.[4] Given time and money (and barring bad luck or faulty research), an editor can, on the other hand, produce an authoritative text, a discussion of the composition and revision of the work and of its production history and reputation, and tables of variant authoritative forms of the text that together make a rich resource for textual study and criticism of a work.

I have already discussed the theoretical concepts bearing on scholarly editions on this scale. I now wish to suggest that, although time and money put limits on what some editors can achieve, these practical constraints do not force us to throw up our hands and do shoddy work simply because ideal work is out of practical reach.

Before editing, before trying to determine how far we will go in our editing effort, we must acknowledge economics: the economics of editing, of book production, and of publishing. Regardless of where our theory of editing may take us, editing is a practical and expensive operation. There is no point in editing a work that is not to be published and no point in publishing a work no one will buy (or subsidize).

The economics of editing is a subject close to home. It involves the editor's time and work assignment. Editing is time-consuming, as any research is. And, like most research, it is done best when it is not constantly interrupted by other, possibly equally important, concerns. The first economic consideration, then, is the editor's workload—the number of classes or students for which the editor, if a teacher, too, is responsible, and the commitments at home and elsewhere. The second is travel. No single library is adequate for an editor's needs. A unique copy of something is always on the other side of the water, if not the world. The third is supplies and equipment: paper, photocopying, microfilm, magnifying glasses, microfilm readers, collating machines (Hinman, Lindstrand, or McLeod), computers, printers, and Internet connections. If the editor has only paper and a pencil, the editorial aims are not very ambitious or the methods not

---

4. Bowers himself corrected his mistake in a paper delivered at the biennial convention of the Society for Textual Scholarship, New York City, Apr. 1985, and incorporated the correction in the paperback version of the Wesleyan edition of *Tom Jones*.

very efficient. In my experience getting the time and the money to do the editing (i.e., obtaining research assignments and travel and supply money) is a significant effort in itself.

But, supposing that the money for an ideal editorial project is at hand, there are other economic factors to consider. Some editors, competent and experienced in editing, know little about modern book production or about alternative forms for distributing texts electronically on compact disks or "on the net." They turn typescripts or word processor files over to a publisher, who after a time provides galley proofs and later page proofs and, finally, a complimentary copy of the finished book or a compact disk. In this age of high technology and shrinking budgets, however, it may be wise to know how a newly edited typescript becomes a book, what costs money, and how the process can affect the edited product.

Although it appears to some that the dawn of electronic publishing has spelled the dusk of print scholarly editions, book publication is not yet dead. Furthermore, book production (the making of the physical objects) needs to be distinguished from publication (directing production and marketing), for a better understanding of these processes may help some editors both conserve money on their projects and increase editorial control over the final products.

The publication process begins with the decision to publish. Copy-editing and book design may be considered part of production, but these activities often take place "in house." When the book is a scholarly edition, publisher and scholar must agree about what parts of the text the copy editor must not touch. Then the publisher decides on design—typefaces, page sizes, format—indicating these matters on the typescript or in a specifications sheet. Often, but not always, the author is invited to review the work of the copyeditor and designer.

Typesetting or composition is the first step of book production. The completed, edited typescript is usually sent to a composing house to be typeset. The process for typesetting most books now is photocomposition —the image of the typepage placed on photographic paper by a computer-driven photocomposer—or laser printing. Most desktop laser printers produce copy at 300dpi (dots per inch), which is not considered book-quality work, but 600dpi and 1200dpi laser printers are comparable in quality to photocomposition. The second job is proofreading by the composing house, the publisher, and the editor, followed by corrections and a new round of proofs. Proofing is done on photocopies of the reproduction proofs or on less-expensive laser print. The layout department provides dummy sheets with page numbers and running heads. So far we are still working with the photographic paper processed by the photocomposer (or photocopies of it).

When final page proofs have been approved and the reproduction proofs are in camera-ready form, the composing work is considered finished. The reproduction proofs, or "mechanicals," are then delivered to the printer, where each page is photographed, producing a large actual-size, high-quality negative film. These negatives are put on a light table, where light spots or scratches are opaqued. The process sometimes also inadvertently removes the tails from commas, the dots from *i*s, or the punctuation from ends of lines. The negatives are then used to create what are called "blues," a final proof form usually provided to the publisher but not usually to the author or editor. Scholarly editors should insist on checking blues; these proofs are the only place to check the results of the work at the light table. Editors should agree with their publishers on a proofing schedule that will make checking blues feasible. At this final proofreading no one in production will forgive an editor who discovers one of his or her own errors, for correction now is very expensive. The negatives are used to burn the plates from which the sheets of the new book are printed.

Although it is generally assumed that nothing can go wrong after final page proofs or blues have been approved, proofreading printed sheets before binding has been known to reveal odd and unfortunate lapses in the production rooms. In the University of South Carolina Press edition of William G. Simms's *Voltmeier* a problem was discovered after sheets were printed that led to the complete reprinting in corrected form of two gatherings. In another incident Fredson Bowers, to his sorrow and that of every Marlowe student, checked neither blues nor unbound sheets of his Cambridge University Press edition of Christopher Marlowe's works, which was published with several pages that had apparently been destroyed and retypeset after final page proofs had been approved by Bowers. Included in the damaged work was the transcription of the alleged unique surviving Marlowe manuscript. A hopeful user—not the reviewers or the editor—discovered the unproofed final work.[5]

The next step in production occurs in the bindery, where even more unfortunate things can happen that will not be known unless every copy of the book is inspected. I have not met any editor whose time and money stretched that far. I remember, however, reading Sir Walter Scott's *Ivanhoe* in a library edition of Scott's works. As I recall, Rebecca and Ivanhoe were

---

5. *Times Literary Supplement*, 26 Apr., 3 May, 10 May 1974.

held captive in a castle beseiged by Cedric and company. The battle raged over the fallen drawbridge, and I looked to the top of the next page only to find myself reading something from the middle of *The Black Dwarf*. The bindery had spoiled the book and the effect; by the time I found my place in another edition I had ceased to care about the fate of Rebecca.

Finally, from the bindery the books go to a distributor—who may or may not be the publisher.

Every step in this process is an expense the publisher bears, although production does not usually take place in the publishing house. What takes place there is a separate expense, but the expenses of both publication and production are the publisher's concern. Publisher's overhead is a famous economic factor. It covers the salaries of a press director and at least one secretary, an acquisitions editor, a copy editor, a designer, and a production manager. It also covers refreshments at the press board meeting at which the decision is made to publish or not to publish the edition proposed. (It is a good idea, by the way, to get some sort of commitment on a proposed edition from a publisher before doing the whole work of the edition.)

What the publisher does is select a potential book, copyedit it, direct its production by several subcontractors—a composing house, a printing house, and a bindery—and arrange for its marketing, perhaps by a distributor. Why they publish is sometimes a mystery. Commercial publishers do it to make money. Consequently, they seldom publish scholarly editions. Academic presses often want to meet the intellectual needs of the academic community, but most of them depend heavily on sales to recover costs, and so they too must watch money carefully. They sometimes will not let the editor do what his editorial principles lead him to desire. They ask, "Who is the intended audience?" (They call it the intended *market*.) They ask, "Shall it be clothbound for the libraries? Paperbound for the classroom?" They try to anticipate the price and perhaps even the heft that the market will bear. And these considerations are taken up independently from the editorial theory followed or the ideals for the treatment of the texts. An editor's perfectly legitimate desire for ancillary material may be pruned by the razor-sharp bottom line in the publisher's budget. So, willy-nilly, our editorial goals are shaped by our economic resources. What we want to do must be meshed with what we can do.

There are two ways to ease the economic pressures that can shape or distort editorial theory and practice. The first is to raise lots of money— enough to cover the costs of what we want to do. The second is to reduce the costs of editing, producing, and publishing the work. I shall not take the time to discuss ways of raising money: grant writing, budget manipulation, thefts, and marriages of convenience are, I suppose, all possibilities. But reductions in costs of editing, producing, and publishing can be accomplished in two ways: limiting the scope and ambition of the edition and taking advantage of modern technology to reduce costs. The second method is, in part, the subject of subsequent chapters.

The first—limiting the scope and ambition of the edition—is worth careful consideration, not because it serves our noblest ideals but because it is often a practical necessity. To put editorial work on a purely cash basis for a moment, the most expensive editorial goal is to provide a critical text (based on detailed comparisons of all potentially authoritative texts), with a textual apparatus (providing the alternative textual forms representing the history of composition and revision) and a critical apparatus (providing background material, biographical and historical contexts for the work)—in short, a rich resource for textual study and analysis of the work. The least expensive editorial goal is to reproduce a preexisting form of a text. Photofacsimile reprints can fulfill such a goal accurately. Remembering that the primary goals of scholarly editing are preservation and restoration, a facsimile at least preserves a historically discrete documentary text and restores it to the user's shelf. Acknowledging that this form of preservation may prolong the life of undesirable features, it at least does not perpetrate new ones—such as usually mark cheap reprints.[6]

What sorts of cuts we are willing to make in our editorial ambitions will depend to a large extent on the need we are trying to meet. Lost or unavailable works might well be simply reprinted, on the grounds that something is better than nothing at all. For example, Henry Kingsley's *The Recollections of Geoffrey Hamlyn* has not been readily available for many years (there was an English edition in 1954). Its inclusion in the Portable Australian Authors series (1982) can be said to be a rescue that provides something where there was nothing—well, not nothing: there was a three-volume first edition in 1859 and a one-volume edition in 1860 (or so the PAA editor says). The Portable Kingsley, however, "rescued" the 1877

---

6. Of course, photoreproductions are not exact copies and may in small but potentially significant ways misrepresent their originals—as has been demonstrated in Frederic Anderson's "Hazards of Photographic Sources," *CEAA Newsletter* 1 (Mar. 1968): 5; Charlyne Dodge, "Photographic Copies vs. Original Documents," *Papers of the Bibliographical Society of America* 71 (1977): 223–26; and D. C. Greetham, *Textual Scholarship: An Introduction* (New York: Garland, 1994), pp. 289–90. However, modern computer digitized images can seem better than originals: see Peter Robinson, *The Digitization of Primary Textual Sources*, no. 4 (Oxford: Office for Humanities Communication Publications, 1993).

reprint because, says the editor in an aside revealing either lack of ambition or lack of funds, it was the earliest one-volume edition "available." What he means by available must be "available given the time and money at his disposal," for his textual note acknowledges the existence somewhere of the earlier (1860) one-volume edition, which was "not available." This "rescue" is limited to such an extent that its scholarly value is questionable.[7]

If the lost work exists only in a badly printed newspaper or a manuscript, unfit for facsimile reproduction, then a straight reprint created with the help of a word processor and computer typesetting might be the most honest "cheap" approach.

On the other hand, a work readily available but only in inadequate or corrupt forms may require more work. We would not be satisfied with another straight reprint of a corrupt text. Even a "less corrupt" reprint would be just another corrupt text. In times of prosperity small gains may be worth something, and superfluity of mediocrity may be tolerable. But hard times make very clear the fact that bad editions drive out good. They are cheaper and easier to produce than good ones, and a superfluity of cheap bad ones makes the economic feasibility of a good one unlikely.

Yet there is middle ground between full-scale editions and mere reprints. Bowers called it the production of practical editions several years ago. One of the finest examples of a series of carefully edited and annotated works produced cheaply is the Colonial Text Series of early Australian texts, the first four volumes of which produced works for which only one form survived.[8] Many classroom texts fall into this category, though the distinction between a mere reprint and a good practical edition as defined by Bowers is often lost in the bookstore. Publishers manage to blur the distinction by making extravagant claims for their mere reprints, and mediocre editors blur the distinction by claiming to do things that they have failed actually to do. Looking, for example, just to the Norton Critical Editions so often used as classroom texts, we find on the covers of all of them the statement "An Authoritative Text." But William Sale's editing of Emily Brontë's *Wuthering Heights* consisted of selecting an edition (not the first)

---

7. Henry Kingsley, *The Recollections of Geoffrey Hamlyn*, intro. by J. S. D. Mellick (St. Lucia: University of Queensland Press, 1982).

8. In particular, Elizabeth Morrison provides a model for such editorial work in her edition of Ada Cambridge, *A Woman's Friendship* (Canberra and Kensington: University of New South Wales Press, 1989), previously published only in the *Age* (Melbourne) newspaper. Morrison provides introductions to the author, the novel, the setting, the phenomenon of newspaper fiction, a rationale for emending single source texts, and annotations that make the book ideal for classroom use.

and reprinting it, while George Ford and Sylvére Monod's editing of Dickens's *Hard Times* consisted of nearly all the work of a full-scale edition. Their text is a critical one; their report on other forms of the work includes the manuscript and revised editions. Sale's "authoritative text" does not deserve to be compared with Ford and Monod's. The blurbs on the covers of a book are usually designed to entice the purchaser, not to describe the contents accurately.

Editing includes not only painstaking research and the execution of editorial decisions but also publishing and book production. The whole process consists of jobs that few persons would any longer undertake without the aid of computers—to create, maintain, alter, and manage text files, to analyze texts with concordance and indexing programs, to compose type for book production, to create hypertext applications, to handle electronic distribution, and to prepare graphic images and print or distribute them electronically. Given proper planning to coordinate the computer use in all areas, any editorial project that involves textual analysis or word processing and that is intended for publication, whether on paper or electronically, can be done more cheaply and more accurately with a computer than without one. Note that I did not say it could be done more easily or more quickly, though that is true of parts of the processes.

Chapter Twelve

Computer-Assisted Scholarly Editing

Each of the five basic approaches to scholarly editing (bibliographical, documentary, sociological, authorial, and aesthetic orientations toward forms) has values that determine the editorial principles to be followed in preparing a text. Although editors tend to appeal to more than one orientation when explaining the editorial solutions to the particular situations they are facing, these orientations are basically incompatible: fulfilling the requirements of one entails the sacrifice of the others. Yet it can be argued that all five are legitimate in the sense that each has developed a more or less internally coherent account of the editing task that includes well-defined notions of what a work of art is and how it is related to extant and potential texts. This leaves the textual editor with the privilege of following the demands of his own formal orientation in preparing the text but with the corollary responsibility of providing an apparatus that will acknowledge and perhaps even suit the needs of students with other orientations as well.

We have, then, several ways to proceed in preparing a scholarly edition—according to one of the five formal orientations with, one can hope, an acknowledgment that some edition users would have preferred another. Regardless of orientation, the editor should want to present the evidence for the whole work, the array of versions that suggests the whole work of art. Aided by computers, editors can provide editions that are genuinely rich resources for literary study, regardless of the editor's formal orientation.[1]

---

1. Portions of this chapter appeared in longer forms in Miriam J. Shillingsburg, "Computer Assistance to Scholarly Editing," *Bulletin of Research in the Humanities* 81 (Winter 1978): 448–63; and Peter Shillingsburg, "The Computer as Research Assistant in Scholarly Editing," *Literary Research Newsletter* 5 (1980): 31–45.

The first job of all editors is to gather relevant variant forms of the work to be edited and, by collation, establish the relationship they bear to one another. Having completed the first step and imposed his will on the text, the editor must prepare printer's copy, first for the newly edited text and then for the apparatus. Then a compositor sets the type, and the editor proofreads. The three most tedious jobs, the ones most liable to careless error, are collation, typesetting, and proofreading. Done with care, these three tasks, frequently described as idiot work because they have a tendency to render workers raving madmen, may prove the most expensive parts of editing.

Scholars engaged in critical editing must do character-for-character comparison of all versions that could conceivably have been authoritatively revised or corrected. Collation forms the groundwork needed to determine, first, what changes occurred during composition of the work or between the time the work left the author's hands and the time it last rolled off the press while the author was living[2] and, second, to determine whether the author, or an editor or compositor, was responsible for those changes. Finally, editors must decide what should be done about those changes in any new edition intended for scholarly audiences. Obviously, for intelligent decisions to be made in these tasks it will take a highly trained literary scholar, thoroughly familiar with the lives, idiosyncrasies, literary works, writing habits, and editorial inclinations of all those persons determined to be the authorizing agents for previous forms of the work. Thanks to computers, collation and proofreading no longer need to take scholars and research assistants such vast amounts of time reading to each other, calling out punctuation marks, spelling words aloud, and recording manually tables of variants with page and line references. The one universal effect of this kind of work is the inducement to sleep. The Center for Editions of American Authors (CEAA) in its *Statement of Editorial Principles* suggested "five or more readings [might be] necessary . . . [although] no precise number of necessary collations can be specified."[3] With a work containing large numbers of dialect spellings, such as Thackeray's *Yellowplush Correspondence,* oral collation is intolerably slow, since most words have to be spelled out. Similarly, where great numbers of variants are found, recording them retards progress unendurably. Although sight collation, verifica-

---

2. Editors of sociological or bibliographic bents may also focus on nonauthorial documents claiming some other type of authority.

3. Center for Editions of American Authors, *Statement of Editorial Principles and Procedures* (New York: Modern Language Association, 1972).

tion, and proofreading will always be necessary as a check, these kinds of editorial tasks have been eased enormously by computer assistance.

The optical machines available to editors before the advent of computers remain necessary and useful in order to compare multiple copies of the same typesetting. The Hinman Collator and the Lindstrand Comparator, which superimpose the images of two copies of the same page so that any variations can be detected by the illusion of a wiggle (in the Hinman machine) or a three-dimensional effect (in the Lindstrand)[4] have been joined by a portable spiderlike device designed by Randall McLeod.[5] But for manuscripts and for different typesettings—and for some editorial projects there may be two to a dozen or even hundreds of variant but potentially authoritative forms—a variety of computer collators have, or can, replace most oral or sight collations.

In oral collation multiple readings have been found necessary because a team of readers is subject to some or all of the following occupational hazards: (1) the oral reader may misread a character in such a way that the listener hears exactly what his text says, (2) the listener may misread a character and thus "see" what he is hearing, (3) alternate "correct" spellings may be passed over because both readers assume the same spelling, (4) the listener's mind wanders, he is distracted momentarily, or he goes to sleep, and (5) one or the other or both collators may be poor spellers and overlook errors because they do not recognize them as such. Once the oral collation is finished one has only a more or less correct list of variants, usually in manuscript form.

When a single human being attempts to compare two texts by looking first at one copy and then at the other, he is perhaps less prone to some of these dangers. But danger 4—daydreaming—is likely aggravated; the single collator works more slowly and risks dizziness and a crick in the neck. If he tries to compare too many words or too long a phrase on each pass, he is liable to memory lapses similar to those of the compositor, who makes word or punctuation or spelling substitutions because of trying to keep in mind too long a passage of copy while setting the type. Using a tape recorder can alleviate some of these problems, but it introduces the added

---

4. Gordon Lindstrand, "Mechanized Textual Collation and Recent Designs," *Studies in Bibliography* 24 (1971): 204–14.

5. See Randall McLeod, "McLeod Portable Collator," *Newsletter, Humanities Association of Canada* 16 (Dec. 1988): 33–41; "Il collazionatore portatile McLeod: una veloce 'collatio' dei testi a stampa come figure," in *La stampa in Italia,* ed. Marco Santoro (Rome, 1992), 325–51. Information also available from McLeod, English Department, University of Toronto, Toronto, Canada M5S 1A1.

disadvantages of forever preserving false starts, ambiguous spellings, and reading errors, which can make subsequent collations in multitext situations slow and perhaps inaccurate.

Another tedious, sleep-inducing labor is the preparation, checking, and rechecking of printer's copy. Then, when the galley and page proofs for the new edition arrive, they likewise have to be checked just as carefully.[6] Hence, the process of producing a scholarly edition of a novel has been long, tedious, expensive, and time-consuming.

A history of early experiments and accomplishments in computer aids to scholarly editing is no longer of much interest, for it has become all one can do to keep up with the new capabilities pouring into our laps.[7]

INPUT

Before a computer can aid the editor, it must be able to "read" the texts; hence, input to computer-readable form is the first task. There are two options, typing and scanning. Scanning is used to produce two very different types of computer files: digital images (graphic images) and searchable text (ASCII) files. The former reproduces the image by giving a digital value to the relative degree of light and dark for each point on a page. Given a high resolution, these digitized images can reproduce very high-quality visual reproductions.[8] As will be seen, graphic images thus produced are extremely

---

6. The Center for Editions of American Authors used to specify that the "proofs must be read at least five times . . . ideally . . . against the original copy-text . . . printer's copy . . . and, if possible, against the other authoritative texts cited in the apparatus."

7. Previous editions contained at this point a brief history of early computer experiments from which I retain only the publications cited: Vinton A. Dearing, "Computer Aids to Editing the Text of Dryden," in *Art and Error: Modern Textual Editing,* ed. Ronald Gottesman and Scott B. Bennet (Bloomington: Indiana University Press, 1970), 254–78; Harold Love, "The Computer and Literary Editing," in *The Computer in Literary and Linguistic Research,* ed. Roy A. Wisbey (Cambridge: Cambridge University Press, 1971), 47–56; Robert L. Oakman, "Textual Editing and the Computer," *Costerus,* n.s. 4 (1975): 79–106; George R. Petty Jr. and William M. Gibson, *Project OCCULT: The Ordered Computer Collation of Unprepared Literary Text* (New York: New York University Press, 1970); Margaret S. Cabaniss, "Using a Computer for Text Collation," *Computer Studies in the Humanities and Verbal Behaviour* 3 (1970): 1–33; Penny Gilbert, "Automatic Collation: A Technique for Medieval Texts," *Computers and the Humanities* 7 (Jan. 1973): 139–47; Robert L. Oakman, "The Present State of Computerized Collation," *Proof* 2 (1972): 345; T. H. Howard-Hill, "A Practical Scheme for Editing Critical Texts with the Aid of a Computer," *Proof* 3 (1973): 335–56; Robert L. Cannon Jr., "OP-COL: An Optimal Text Collation Algorithm," *Computers and the Humanities* 10 (Jan. 1976): 33–40.

8. See Robinson, *The Digitization of Primary Textual Sources,* no. 4 (Oxford: Office for Humanities Communication Publications, 1993), for a very specific and practical survey of

important in electronic editions; for use in computerized text comparison, however, digitized texts are useless. Scanners can also produce "readable" texts by programs designed to recognize characters and convert their images to ASCII equivalents. This is a delicate and complicated procedure susceptible to error and frustration in several ways. The best scanners can be "taught" to recognize almost any type font in almost any type size with almost any amount of leading or white space between words. However, among the things that even the best scanners continue to stumble over is foxing (rust stains), bleeding (ink seepage through the leaf, obscuring text on the obverse side), poor alignment along the baseline, and badly worn, blunted, or broken type. These troublesome characteristics are common to older books and cheaply manufactured modern books. Since older texts are what most editors have to work with, these limitations render scanning unsatisfactory for most editorial projects. Nevertheless, some projects use scanned texts as a check against the quite different disadvantages of input by typing; scanners tend to goof by producing nonsense, typists tend to goof in ways that look plausible. Yet, a good typist can still input text more accurately and cheaply from older books than a scanner can because good typists make fewer errors. Moreover, optical scanners are not practical for manuscripts of the sort that literary editors have to deal with.[9]

There are, nevertheless, drawbacks to any input method that requires an operator to type in information. The files produced by the retyping of texts are subject to three types of infidelity: typing errors that are unique to a specific typing job (i.e., other typings of the same passage are different); typing errors that agree with some but not all other editions; and typing errors that alter the copy in the same way that all other editions also alter it. The first two kinds of infidelity are much more likely than the last (i.e., it is less likely that all typists and compositors will introduce by accident precisely the same error than that at least some will get it right, or, if all get it wrong, that they will not all get it wrong in the same way). And

---

the capabilities and problems in this area. Available from Oxford Computing Services, 13 Banbury, Oxford, England OX2 6NN.

9. The idea of scanning and then running a spell-checker to catch scanning errors (recommended by Peter Robinson in "Collation, Textual Criticism, Publication, and the Computer," *Text* 7 [1994]: 84) is dangerously prone to "correct" errors and eccentricities actually in the source text, rendering the computer version an inaccurate witness. On the same page Robinson suggests that files representing other manuscripts can be created by altering an existing file for another manuscript. Perhaps there are situations in which that would be safe but not in any I'm familiar with. One would have to collate and discover every variant *before* creating the computer file representing the manuscript.

the more common situations are much less dangerous. Unique typing errors and typing alterations that disagree with at least one other text will be discovered by the computer collation and printed out as variants. One checking of the variants printout against the original texts uncovers all the first two kinds of errors. The only errors remaining will be instances in the original that differ from all subsequent texts but that the typist altered to *agree* with all subsequent texts. Likewise, the only undetected variants in the originals of the other texts will be instances in which these texts have unique readings that the typist accidentally altered to agree with all other texts. The computer can never discover this kind of transcription error, but errors of the first two types and all legitimate variants can be detected by computer collation.[10]

INTEGRATED SYSTEMS OF COMPUTER ASSISTANCE

Computer collation and computer-driven photocomposition are now practical realities in scholarly publishing. The simple act of putting these two major computer-related editorial activities together in one connected process bore astonishing but now quite commonplace results. A good computer-assisted process has certain basic characteristics: First, it is an integrated system in which the output from any one stage of computer work is usable as input for the next stage. What this really means is that a good system requires input for each documentary text just one time and that all output of text and apparatus could be generated without rekeying any part of the text. That being the case, every error detected and corrected during the research and editing process is an error that does not need to be caught while proofreading the results of typesetting.[11]

Second, a good process starts with the initial examination of source texts and carries through to the typesetting and printing of the end product,

---

10. The Greek Thesaurus project at the University of California, Irvine, contracted with its typists for files with only one error per twenty-five-thousand keystrokes; because the Thackeray project is based on text comparison that finds errors automatically, it can tolerate a higher error rate in initial input. Of course, the better the typist, the more efficient is the process, but one error per fifteen-thousand keystrokes is easily acceptable for working copies. See Petty and Gibson, *Project OCCULT,* 37; and Ben R. Schneider Jr. *Travels in Computerland; or, Incompatibilities and Interfaces* (Reading, Mass.: Addison-Wesley, 1974), 117–47.

11. Having completed all the collations and verifications of the computer work for an edition of *Henry Esmond* without sight collating any text (except the manuscript against our printout of it), we performed a careful sight collation of our corrected computer file against the five-hundred-page first edition and found one error the machine had missed—a turned letter that the typist had entered as if it had been correct.

saving time and money and improving the accuracy of the final product at every stage.

Third, nothing of a mechanical or repetitive nature is of necessity done by hand and eye. That is, good computer programs minimize or eliminate the "idiot work."

Fourth, every stage in the process is interruptable, reviewable, revisable, and, if necessary, repeatable. This important aspect of computer assistance needs emphasis but can be overemphasized. Editing is an art, not a science, and computers are only machines. As editors, we do not want our decisions to be influenced by the limitations of the tools we use. Any artist or craftsman worth his salt who lacks a tool to do a certain thing gets or makes one that will.

There are several integrated systems for computer-assisted scholarly editing: PC-CASE, available for use on DOS, is described in a coda to this chapter. Its sophisticated offspring, MAC-CASE, is a hypertext version developed for use on Macintosh equipment.[12] TUSTEP, the process used to produce an edition of James Joyce's *Ulysses,* is available in German and runs on DOS machines.[13] An integrated system developed by Thomas Faulkner, working in the English Department at Washington State University on an edition of Robert Burton's *Anatomy of Melancholy*, is little known, for, though he has described the general capabilities of the programs at conferences, I have seen it described only briefly in print.[14] Similarly, the Center for Editing Early Canadian Texts (CEECT), under the direction of Mary Jane Edwards, uses an integrated series of programs known collectively as PROOF and DUMBO/TIMOTHY "to take our texts through eleven steps from their first entry in the wordprocessor to their exit as a tape produced for the printer."[15]

COLLATE, developed by Peter Robinson at the Oxford University Computing Service, is the most sophisticated of the integrated systems now

---

12. Information on MAC-CASE is available from Paul Eggert, English Department, University College, ADFA, Campbell, ACT 2600, Australia.

13. James Joyce, *Ulysses: A Critical and Synoptic Edition,* ed by Hans Walter Gabler, with Wolfhard Steppe and Claus Melchior (New York: Garland Publishing, 1984). TUSTEP is described in Francisco Marcos Marín, "Computers and Text Editing," *Romance Philology* 45 (1991): 102–22.

14. Dean Guenther et al., "TEX at Washington State University," *TUGboat* 5, no. 1 (1984): 24–25.

15. Mary Jane Edwards, "Angles from the Margin: Editing Early English-Canadian Literature," in *Editing in Australia*, Occasional Paper no. 17, English Department, University College ADFA, ed. Paul Eggert (Kensington: University of New South Wales Press, 1990), 95.

available. It handles either prose or verse, processes multiple versions at once, and automates significant amounts of encoding for printing or for electronic distribution (about which there is more in a chap. 14, "Electronic Editions"). It runs on Macintosh machines.[16]

COLLATION

Comparison of texts from manuscripts and from different editions cannot be done mechanically. Collation was the first major accomplishment of electronic assistance to scholarly editing. Pioneering efforts are described in the papers listed in note 6. The most successful programs are still useful: the Donne Variorum Collation Program, developed by Gary Stringer from the collation programs created by Vinton Dearing for the University of California Dryden project, are restricted to use with poetry; they run on DOS machines and handle up to a hundred texts at once.[17] UNITE, developed in Spain and available in both Spanish and English, is said to have the most user-friendly interface but is also restricted to use with verse and has heavy, precollation preparation requirements.[18] URICA, developed at the University of South Carolina, is an interactive program alerting typists of new texts when they have typed a variant to a designated preexisting text file or allowing an editor to move from variant to variant within already input texts; its output is not designed for reuse as input to some further editorial task, and its usefulness is limited to small projects.

DATA MAINTENANCE AND MANIPULATION

Like the gathering of relevant texts, collation is basic investigatory research. It must be completed before editing begins. When collation is finished, the editor has corrected computer files representing each authoritative text and computer collations of all of them. Computer-assisted scholarly editing from this point on is a matter of data manipulation and record maintenance. Decisions remain to be made about how to emend, how to record variants, and how to present both text and apparatus.

---

16. Manuals in information available from the OUCS, 13 Banbury Road, Oxford, England OX2 6NN. See also Robinson, "Collation," 77–94.

17. The Donne Collation program is reviewed by Ray Siemens, "Textual Collation Software for the PC: PC-CASE, UNITE, and the Donne Variorum Collation Program," *Text Technology* 4 (1994): 209–13.

18. Siemens, 213–17. For a more extensive review of UNITE, see Francisco Marcos Marín, "Computers and Text Editing," *Romance Philology* 45 (1991): 102–22. See also Robinson, "Collation," 85 n.

In the days when typewriters and pens were the editor's main tools, decisions once made tended to stay made. It was frequently too difficult to imagine the job of revising a mountain of work in response to some minor change of mind about how the editing should have gone. With the aid of CASE programs for the Thackeray edition, I found that the ease with which an editorial decision can be reversed or tried in some new way and then restored had the disadvantage of making all decisions seem temporary; some decisions were taken a second or third time. Vacillating editors must be careful lest they never finish.

A good computer-assisted process gives editors added control over quality, since the collation process is also a process for detecting errors in the file that sets the type for the new edition. Further control is gained over more of the book production process, since it is the editor and not the printer who effects corrections in the file to be typeset. And it can be the editor, instead of the printer, who incorporates aspects of design and copyediting agreed upon with the publishers.

Another ancient fear among editors contemplating computers was that mechanization would render editing mechanical. Now the fear is that editors might assume the computer can do more than it really can. Both the fearful and the overeager must remember that the computer is only an assistant to the editor. It does no editing. Its prodigious capacity to do menial tasks endlessly and accurately makes it the editor's dream assistant, not the editor's replacement. The editor must tell the computer in detail what to do and when to do it. After each task is completed by the computer, the editor must still decide what to do with the data and how to use it. If scholarly editing were big business, there would be canned programs for every conceivable repetitive or data-manipulating task that editing involves. Instead, we have a small but growing number of highly specialized programs.

Two important points about computer-assisted editing are worth emphasizing here. The first is that the process is "interactive"; that is, the editor performs some task and turns the process over to the computer, which quickly and accurately performs a tedious, repetitious task and gives it back to the editor, who decides what to do about the material and turns it back to the computer, and so on. Computer assistance is just assistance; the editor remains the master. But that brings up the second point: a master must know what he is doing and how to do it. The computer is a mindless slave doing just what it is told, and, if it does not do what one expected it to do, that is because one did not tell it precisely what to do.

Among the important advantages of computer-assisted editing is that once the text in magnetic form is "edited" (and checked by humans), it will stay edited during the publication process, because the files generated and corrected by the editorial process are used to run the typesetting machine. Furthermore, if at a late stage in the checking, one finds errors that previously would have necessitated either extensive retyping of printer's copy or, in rare cases, extensive resetting of type, an editor can make these changes easily, accurately, and rapidly in the computer file at the editorial office. No one would have to look "by hand" for all occurrences of the error to be corrected, and extensive proofreading would not have to be redone. Hence, the real saving is in greatly reduced proofreading and press correction at the galley and page proof stages. In theory, since there is no human intervention, there should be no errors introduced between the time the editor turns the electronic file of his text over to the publisher and the time the book reaches the bindery. That process is not automatic. While only a foolish editor would trust the machine to get it right the first time, a single proofreading will probably suffice or at least be enough to indicate whether more would be necessary. By any standard, though, this process of integrating research, editing, and proofing in one continuous operation is more accurate than conventional typesetting. It has revolutionized scholarly editing and publishing. The reduction in busywork on the editor's part makes multivolume editions of Victorian triple-deckers a realistic goal.

Like word processing, and unlike collation, indexing is a computer task with a large constituency, and, therefore, the options in software are significant. Many of the major word processing packages come with indexing components, and a glance at the *Computer User's Directory, 1994–1995,* produced by the Technology Committee of the Association for Documentary Editing, shows that a significant number of the editorial projects surveyed rely upon them. In addition, CINDEX, Clipper, DataPerfect, dBaseIII, Double Helix, FoxPro FrameMaker, Indexx, InMagic, MicroIndex, Excel, Microsoft Works, Paradox, PFS Professional File, and Word-Cruncher are actively used for indexing on specific projects.

Editors may wish to use a concordance program to give fast access to lexically related parts of a text. The Oxford Concordance Program, for example, can, from the text file, produce (1) a list, alphabetically arranged, of all the words in the text with line number and context, (2) a simple index with the line numbers for each word, or (3) an alphabetical list of the vocabulary used for the work, with the number of times each word is use in the text. Other concordance programs can do these things as well. With this computer tool the editor can at least know whether a decision to emend in one place may also necessitate, for consistency's sake, an emendation somewhere else. (I am not suggesting that consistency is of itself desirable.) Concordance programs are also useful in identifying patterns and ranges of usage, which editors might find more useful than impressions gained by reading and rereading the texts to be edited to help form notions of an author's or publisher's or compositor's habits. The Oxford Concordance Program is perhaps the most widely used concordance program.

Finally, there is a host of off-the-shelf software programs editors might find useful in their work but that are not peculiar to editorial projects using computers. These include virus protection, file backup, spreadsheets, file conversion programs, data compression, disk management, mail mergers, graphics tools, and general utilities packages. I reserve mention of software relative to typesetting, hypertext, multimedia, and Internet access to later chapters.

The project is completed when its research is completed, its editorial decisions made and recorded, its text prepared for publication, its apparatus constructed, the editor's introductions and notes on the text added, and the headnotes for the tables inserted. Or is it completed? All that editors "in the old days" did is done except the proofreading. The computer files could at this time produce "hard copy" which, I suppose, could be sent to the publisher for traditional publication. But I cannot imagine an editor with accurate, proofread, computer-readable text files allowing a typesetting house to rekey texts. Instead, the next step is to use these files to run the typesetting equipment. With this capability all the added expense of computer-assisted editing pays off. In combining the editorial process with the book production system, all the care scholars lavished on the preparation of compositor's copy serves the added function of verifying the typesetting input. Compositor's copy is, in effect, an advanced stage of proofs. Properly prepared and handled, the editor's files can be fed directly into a computer typesetting device, bypassing compositors and thus bypassing the major source for error and alteration in book production. The preparation of setting copy and composition for typesetting are united in one operation in properly integrated systems.

Under normal printing house conditions, changes in the typesetting, the film, or the reproduction prints are always necessary. Normal practice is to seek out errors by proofreading and to change them during and after typesetting. Major corrections may require rekeying parts of the text; minor changes are effected by stripping in the corrections on camera-ready copy or film negatives. Of course, these normal correction processes also provide the opportunity for introducing new textual errors. But error-free original input to the photocomposer in order to avoid the normal processes of rekeying and stripping in corrections is precisely what a computerized editorial process must and can accomplish.

COMPUTER-ASSISTED SCHOLARLY EDITING: AN EXAMPLE

What follows is a brief survey of the PC-CASE programs. PC-CASE is not the only integrated system of programs designed to help editors from original text investigation through a variety of editorial tasks to typesetting, but it is the one I know best. CASE programs were designed for use with very long prose texts for which there are up to eight variant texts.[19] CASE programs are available or have been available to run on mainframes of various sorts (Univac, Prime, Dec, Vax, and IBM) and on DOS machines and the Macintoshes. PC-CASE runs on DOS and is menu driven. It consists of a battery of nine separate programs for a variety of manuscript- and text-related editorial activities. It is not a word processor nor a typesetter; it does not index or concord texts. It does not encode texts automatically for typesetting or for universal electronic distribution. All of these are necessary or helpful computer-related activities for which an editor will need specific software. PC-CASE is an aid to transcription, collation, verification, and apparatus development such that the initial keying or scanning of each source text is the first and only heavily manual, error-prone activity. All subsequent text development or manipulation acts are computer aided and designed to improve the accuracy of the edition materials. Output from the PC-CASE programs is designed to be input for typeset or electronic editions.

As already mentioned, word processors that deal routinely with text-only or ASCII files are preferred because not only CASE but most other text-handling programs, such as typesetters, electronic text presentation programs, and concordances, require text-only input. PC-CASE disregards all formatting and font commands embedded as blind control characters.

---

19. For verse texts COLLATION is more appropriate. For prose texts with more than eight authoritative forms COLLATION may be better than dealing with small groups of texts in PC-CASE, but for long texts, such as Victorian novels, COLLATION required preliminary analysis not necessary with PC-CASE. Nevertheless, COLLATION offers other capabilities not offered in PC-CASE, and editors with access to Macintoshes would do well to investigate its advantages.

PC-CASE provides three general categories of programs: (1) for manuscript manipulation, (2) for collation, and (3) for apparatus building.[20] The first step in the process is to create computer-readable files of the source texts by typing them into the computer with a text editor according to certain input specifications.[21] These specifications are simple enough, and most of the typing is like any other kind of typing. It is essential to specify the beginnings of paragraphs and to keep lines from exceeding eighty characters in length. It is desirable to indicate where pages begin and to reproduce the line configuration of the source text so that page and line numbers are automatically developed, for the text file will match the page and line number of the text it represents. Inputting codes for typesetting or for electronic distribution makes very good sense from the very beginning. Fonts, formats, and structures that are significant in the final versions of the work should be indicated from the beginning so that the verification process can improve their accuracy as well as the accuracy of the text.[22]

Once two texts are available in the computer, collation can begin. The collation proceeds through a series of startup programs that run one after the other as long as no impossible situations caused by faulty input are encountered. The purpose of the temporary files thus created is to provide page and line numbers in the output and to identify a series of matching points throughout the text to which the program can resort when very large variants interrupt the routine comparison of similar texts.

The result of collation is a file of variants, each labeled according to source text with page and line number. If in the process of collation a very large divergence is encountered, such as when a page or paragraph or chapter is added, deleted, or transposed, the collation program temporarily declares itself lost, skips to the next matching startpoint and backs up until it is lost again—thus reducing to as small a portion as possible the problem passage for the editor to sort out manually. Then the program moves to the startpoint again and proceeds in the ordinary manner.

The result of collation is a computer file whose appearance is dictated in part by the fact that it will be used as input for additional text manipu-

---

20. For a history of development, see M. J. Shillingsburg, "Computer Assistance," 448–63; P. L. Shillingsburg, "Computer as Research Assistant," 31–45.

21. See *Guide to PC-CASE: Computer Assisted Scholarly Editing for Micro-Computers* vers. 2.1 (Mississippi State University, 1987), for the details.

22. All anticipated codes that cannot be generated automatically by tagging programs should be input from the start. For this purpose many projects develop a simplified set of mnemonic codes for the limited number of markings needed. Then a conversion program is developed, or a search-and-replace routine with a word processor converts to the (usually) longer codes actually wanted.

lation. If a presentable hard copy is desired, the PC-CASE menu offers a print program with results illustrated in Fig. 1.

```
M0019012 most brilliant ( colours ) and youthful
C0012009 most brilliant ( colors ) and youthful
M0019023 had told ( Stycorax ) that her
C0012018 had told ( Sycorax ) that her
M0019024 very fine ( man.) ) that praise
C0012019 very fine ( man) ) that praise
M0019030 a Jacobite ( like ) his father
C0013001 a Jacobite ( as ) his father
```

Fig. 1. Raw variants list, output from the initial collation, showing the differences between the master text and one comparison text.

When the source text is a manuscript, the scholarly editor usually wants a record of the alterations (the cancelations, write-overs, and insertions) as well as a record of the variants between the final manuscript text and subsequent printed texts. For these needs PC-CASE has manuscript manipulation programs. The input specifications for manuscripts include a system for indicating canceled, overwritten, and inserted material. (See Fig. 2.)

```
The idea [had over was] been familiar to her mind when
she yet wore pinafores, and when Harry, the dirtiest
of little boys |used to| [come over came] back with
black eyes from school to Drummington|;| or to his
fathers /neighbouring\ |house of Logwood|, where
Lady Ann lived much with her aunt.
```

Fig. 2. Sample of a diplomatic translation incorporating cancellations (between slashes), insertions (between uprights), and writeovers (within square brackets).

A printout of the diplomatic transcription should be proofread against the original manuscript, since transcriptions are most often created from photoreproductions and because transcriptions are technically complex enough to make input errors more likely. Once proofed and updated, the manuscript file is automatically transformed into a fair-copy file by a program that strips out all canceled passages, editorial commentary, and symbols indicating manuscript alterations. The result is a clear text file that can be collated against other source text files. Actually, a diplomatic transcription can be collated against another text, providing a list of alterations and variants in one (usually large) file.

Another program run on the diplomatic transcription of the manuscript produces a file of alterations in the text beginning with a page and line number, then a pickup word and the altered text, in the format illustrated by Fig. 3.

```
4.1 idea [had over was] been
4.3 boys |used to| [come over came] back
4.4 to Drummington|;| or
4.4 fathers /neighbouring\ |house of Logwood|, where
```

Fig. 3. List of alterations in manuscript

When all the collations have been run, verified, and corrected, the first major work of research assistance by computer is finished. There is now an accurate computer-readable file of the base text of the work, and there is an accurate variants list file, or two or three, revealing the textual differences among the source texts. The next major step is editorial. No machine can decide which version of the work to present as the clear reading text. But there is a convenient paper printout on which the editor can record his emendations and keep track of the sources for the emendations.

Having decided on the emendations, the editor makes a copy of the file representing the copy-text, with which to create an emended text file. A computer collation of the copy-text file with the emended file will produce a complete and accurate list of emendations.

Another set of programs was developed to generate the edition's apparatus. The conflation program takes three or four or more variants lists that represent savable, recordable variants (as illustrated in Fig. 1) and merges them into a single list (illustrated in Fig. 4). Each variant is labeled by page and line for the base text or master text and, to the right, by the sigla for texts containing that reading. If the list contains information too trivial to record, the editor simply goes through the list file deleting unwanted entries. If some entries belong in one table of the apparatus while others belong elsewhere, the editor goes through the whole list labeling the entries

```
M0010012 most brilliant ( colours ) and youthful ]E1 R53
         most brilliant ( colors ) and youthful ]NY TCH
M0019023 had told ( Stycorax ) that her    ]E1
         had told ( Sycorax ) that her     ]NY TCH
         had told ( Sicorax ) that her     ]R53
M0019024 very fine ( man,) ) the praise    ]E1 TCH
         very fine ( man) ) the praise     ]NY R53
M0019030 a Jacobite ( like ) his father    ]E1
         a Jacobite ( as ) his father      ]NY TCH R53
```

Fig. 4. Printout format for a conflation. Sigla after the bracket indicate editions corresponding to the reading on that line.

according to the tables he wants to build; a program creates the separate tables for him.

Since publishers want to save space, the entries in Fig. 4 are reduced to look like those in Fig. 5 by a program designed to strip away the extra material found useful in working drafts.

```
M0019012 colours    ]E1 R53
         colors     ]NY TCH
M0019023 Stycorax   ]E1
         Sycorax    ]NY TCH
         Sicorax    ]R53
M0019024 man,)      ]E1 TCH
         man)       ]NY R53
M0019030 like       ]E1
         as       ]NY TCH R53
```

Fig. 5. Printout format for conflation without pickup words.

The next step is to embed encoding, either for typesetting or for electronic distribution. If original input and editorial updating was done with an eye to this next step in the process, then short mnemonic codes developed for the specific needs of the project are already embedded in the computer files. In that case a simple conversion program will change project codes to appropriate typesetting codes or codes for electronically distributed texts (such as TEI conformant SGML codes), for which see chapters 13 and 14.

Chapter Thirteen

Computer Typesetting

My interest in computer typesetting arose primarily because I had computer files produced with CASE for a scholarly edition and a desire to set them in type in such a way that the likelihood of introducing new errors would be minimized, but one does not need the CASE programs in order to generate computer files for typesetting. The procedures in this chapter are applicable to any computer file destined for print. My remarks are based on the experiences I have had providing two books on computer disk to two university presses, providing camera-ready copy for four volumes of the Thackeray edition to Garland Publishing, providing camera-ready copy for the Norton Critical Edition of *Vanity Fair,* and negotiating the production process of the third edition of this book. I have used three different versions of Donald Knuth's TEX typesetting programs and have dealt with four different composing houses that provided TEX output by photocomposition and by laser printers. I have corresponded with and visited several composing houses in the United States and England while exploring possibilities for typesetting the Thackeray edition, and I have advised other editors with regard to their use of computer files as input to composing houses chosen by their publishers. What follows here is a general introduction to the procedures an editor might follow and an outline of the kinds of knowledge needed in order to succeed in meshing editorial work with the demands of book production. Some of this may seem complicated to the neophyte, but the rewards in reduced costs and increased accuracy make learning these procedures well worth the effort.

There are two major areas to consider when providing computer files as typesetting input. The first involves craftsmanship and design and the ability to attend to the details of the typesetting and book designing trades—page formatting, character sets, fonts, leading, serifs, kerning, ligatures, footnotes, headers, chapter and section headings, block indentations, justification, end-of-line hyphenation, and spacing adjustments for italic type. The second involves negotiating with and working with a publisher and a composing house director over who does what, who is responsible for what, who pays for what, and how the work gets done.

CAMERA-READY COPY

Recent advances in word processing have blurred the line between sophisticated word processing and low-end desktop publishing. Consequently editors and other scholars have undertaken to give their publishers camera-ready copy. But there is a palpable and, for many, an important difference in quality and meaning between texts prepared on word processors and those prepared with desk-top publishing packages and there is a further distinction of importance to be made between desktop publishing and full-scale typesetting programs. In part these distinctions stem from varying capabilities of text-handling programs; in part they stem from differences in the print quality of the output.

Word processors, more and more, try to approximate the grace and dexterity of professional typesetting. Multiple type fonts in multiple sizes, proportional spacing, justified margins, integration of graphics, variable pitch, automatic footnoting, headers, footers, columns, and indexing are common to most of the major programs. Combined with laser printing, the results can be very impressive and "will do" to satisfy many. The question may be, would we rather see a particular, very useful scholarly tool in print, or would our demands for quality in appearance (as well as research and accuracy) justify an indeterminate delay in production? The appearance of many scholarly books indicates that immediate publication is more important to many than the aesthetics of the print media.

This condition is a shame, in my opinion, for not only are inexpensive options easily available to do better; scholarly editions are also too important to be reduced to inelegant, expedient half-measures. Proponents of the bibliographic orientation have demonstrated beyond argument, I believe, that the appearance of books signifies a range of important meanings to their users. Many scholarly works produced on word processors look cheap and convey a sense of ephemerality or tawdriness or general insufficiency about the book, which unfortunately frequently attaches to the work represented by the book.

Desktop publishing packages have begun to address these problems by introducing some of the niceties of professional composition. Programs such as PageMaker, Ventura, and Author (none of which I have used myself) advance the concept of page layouts and formatting generally. They also offer subtleties in fonts such as kerning (providing a more aesthetic juxtaposition of letters that slant or have overhangs like j, y, and f, particularly in their italic forms [*fj* or *Fjord*, e.g.]) and ligatures for f i and f l (fi and fl). But, frequently, their method of avoiding widows or clubs (paragraphs with one opening line at the bottom of the page or a single closing line at the top of the next) is to truncate the page or leave noticeable extra space between paragraphs or to revise the text.

Full-scale typesetting programs, however, offer infinite gradations of spacing between lines and between words so that widows and clubs can be avoided in ways that do not require textual revision and that are imperceptible to the reader. They provide a full range of ligatures for ff, ffl, ffi and, in some fonts, *fg, fs, ft,* and *ct* combinations, kerning that can be adjusted, automatic footnoting, running headlines, pagination, and paragraph shaping to wrap around illustrations, charts, and figures.

In developing the design of a book, professional book producers also bring a trained eye to the type density of pages, a sense of the fonts with appropriate weight and, one might say, connotation for the material being presented. The length of lines and number of lines per page is dictated, to some extent, by the economies of page size, but not entirely. The degree of indentation for paragraphs, blocked material, letter headings and salutations, signatures, and charts are all matters that can be thought about and controlled or left to the default settings of the programs being used.

The print quality of laser printers, besides being determined by type font choices and the type density of the pages, is usually measured in "resolution" by the number of "dots per inch" printed. Most laser printers of the 1980s were 300dpi and, by comparison with dot matrix and typewriter printers, produced amazing results. In the 1990s, 600dpi laser printers became affordable and have been cited as adequate for commercial printing by some scholarly presses. Yet, among professional compositors, who had become accustomed to the sharp quality of photocomposition, 1200dpi is considered barely adequate. The problem at the base of this array of opinions can be easily seen, even by untrained eyes, with the aid of a magnifying glass to examine the slanted lines of letters such as x, w, v, M, N, Y, K, and z and the curved lines of s, c, a, e, B, P, G, D, and others, for where the lines are neither vertical nor horizontal the lower-quality output has a stairstep outline. The result in print for normal reading is a faint fuzziness that might be nearly imperceptible in the original laser output but that becomes increasingly vague in the reproductions necessary for mass printing.

Two reasons, then, might prompt editors to send computer-readable files on disks to the publisher, instead of camera-ready copy: the editor neither has to learn the intricacies of book design, layout, or typesetting nor has to own high-quality programs and printers. Publishers usually hire out the preparation of camera-ready copy to a composing house with commercial-quality equipment.

NEGOTIATING WITH PUBLISHERS

I skip the negotiations over contracts, schedules of submission, and royalties, to the details of book production. Authors and editors with interest and expertise in book production can be seen by publishers as threats of unwanted encroachment on the traditional domain of skilled artisans in publishing and composing houses. Therefore, editors wishing themselves to handle any parts of book production traditionally handled by the publisher, or by commercial services, should be prepared for interpersonal reactions that are hard to predict or to generalize about. But perhaps that is the best place to start.

Traditionally, the author or editor provided typed sheets to a publisher, who handled or arranged for production. I presume one can use the past tense for that now, even though for many authors and editors the typed sheets might now be printouts from computers. It is now common, however, to supply publishers with the texts on disk along with the hard copy, though it remains the case that some publishers and journal editors are not prepared to handle computer files and may be ignorant of what is involved. Publishers traditionally select manuscripts for publication, copyedit them, and provide specifications for the design of the book—that is, they specify the size of each page, the amount of margin, the type font and size, the contents of the running headlines, the style and size of title page and chapter titles, the location and type size for notes, and captions for illustrations. They also worry about widows and orphans, tight and loose lines, and anything that affects the readability and aesthetic look of the printed pages. Dust jacket copy and binding specifications are also their concern, but we will leave that for now. None of the publisher's work *requires* a computer. (I was told once that the only equipment a publisher really needs can be found in a telephone booth.) If the author has provided a clean, double-spaced, typed printer's copy, then copyediting and design notes can be penciled in and the paper sent to the composing house, where, for the first time in the traditional process, a computer is used. So, the author/editor with a computer file for publication may have to take the publisher by the hand and lead the negotiations with the director of a composing house willing and able to accept computer files. And both publisher and compositor may need to be persuaded about the author/editor's production competence. This situation is, fortunately, now justly endangered; most publishers have developed some level of computer literacy.

A good procedure to follow is to give the publisher a printout (preferably a traditionally formatted printout without visible printer's codes) for use in copyediting and book design. The publisher should then, contrary to tradition, return the marked copy to the author/editor to have the computer files updated accordingly. One might note that this process guarantees the author/editor an opportunity to intervene at an early stage if the copy editor has overzealously interfered with significant material. There is the frightening remembrance of what the Oxford University Press did to the Shelley *Journals*. In the printer's copy the editor, Paula Feldman, made a distinction between Shelley's own dashes (which she rendered as em-dashes) and editorial dashes (which she rendered as en-dashes). The copy editor, failing to note the distinction or not appreciating the importance of it, regularized all dashes to em-dashes. By the time the editor found out what had been done, the book was already set in type and the job of restoring the en-dashes was deemed too expensive by the press. Repair being denied, other adjustments and compromises had to be pursued to mitigate the damage. Intervention by the scholar/editor after the publisher's copyediting but before typesetting seems a very good idea. Some university presses, realizing the importance of this step, routinely have authors review the copy editor's work.

Once the publisher's wishes have been incorporated in the computer file, a new printout and the computer file can be sent to the composing house for typesetting. The printout this time should be a "dump" of the computer file, complete with typesetting codes. Any elements of design for which the author/editor was unable to introduce codes should be described so that the compositor can add them.

Unfortunately, this process has complicating factors that I have skated over: communications between the editor's computer and the composing house computer and differences in typesetting software. These are becoming less and less of a problem, but they must be attended to. The author must use a word processor compatible with that of the publisher or composing house, or one for which the composing house has a conversion program, or must supply text-only (ASCII) files. This can be put a different way: the composing house chosen must be able to accept and read the computer files the author/editor has produced. The technology of typesetting grew up before, and independently from, word-processing technology, and many computer typesetting machines are unable to take as input anything that was not keyed in either at the input terminal for that machine or another one of the same brand. Each of these problems has become minimal, but a publisher trying to save money by using a garage typesetter can still throw a monkey wrench into the smooth coordination of the editor-publisher-compositor negotiations and operations. An author or editor should ask to talk directly with the composing house computer wizard to establish whether the files can be electronically mailed (e-mailed) or should be submitted on a particular kind of floppy disk.

So much for basic communication of files between editor and compositor. The next problem is the typesetting software. I am assuming here that the editor has chosen not to produce camera-ready copy with a desktop publishing package but to go, instead, with the full-scale capabilities of commercial typesetting. The only desktop package that approaches commercial typesetting is Donald Knuth's TEX, which has some relatively user-friendly implementations, such as LaTEX. What follows applies both to TEX typesetting (done in the editor's workshop) and commercial typesetting from files containing generic codes.

TYPESETTING AND ORIGINAL RESEARCH

As early as possible, the typesetting process to be used should be identified specifically. Various typesetting software systems share many similarities, but there are differences as well. The editor has a choice of setting up computer files with specific typesetter software in mind or of providing generic codes. Each choice has its advantages. For example, the editor who has chosen to work with TEX has a specific list of predetermined codes to use, described in the TEX manual. Additional codes for special effects can be constructed in the language of TEX. Like most typesetting systems, TEX has a shorthand system for specific jobs. It involves setting up a macro package, a set of preliminary directions to the typesetter for all sorts of routine formatting demands. A good macro package will provide short memorable names for recurring situations so that, for example, when one reaches the end of a chapter and wishes to begin a new chapter, a single command such as "chapterhead" or "%ch" can be used instead of a series of commands that will stand for the codes that mean end of paragraph, do not justify the last line, end of page, do not stretch the page out to fill all the white space, start a new page, skip down x amount of space at the top of the page, specify the normal chapter head fonts, and do not put a running headline or a page number on this page. It is always easier to use macros than to write them.

But an editor need not learn TEX commands or those for any other typesetting program. A keen sense of the font and formatting demands of typesetting generally is sufficient in developing a simple generic set of codes that can later be converted to TEX or to any other set of codes for printing or for electronic distribution, as we shall see. So, if an editor has used TEX commands or generic ones in the text and then finds that the publisher has chosen a composing house that uses the Penta System or some other typesetting software, the composing house has a small problem to overcome. It is one that would have been avoided had the same system been used that was anticipated from the beginning. Every TEX or generic command will have to be changed to a command of the chosen system. The solutions are simple. At the low-tech end, a word processor with a search-and-change command can make the necessary substitutions in a few easy steps. In the long run a more efficient way is for a programmer to write an ad hoc substitution program in which a list of the specific commands used can be replaced by the equivalent commands from another system. There will probably be a few changes that have to be made one at a time. One system I worked with for the Thackeray edition, for example, required a code only at the end of a line to be centered, whereas TEX requires one both before and after the centered material. A thoughtfully written substitution program can handle even such situations automatically.

The editor may choose to prepare the text with generic codes, leaving to the publisher the choice of typesetting system and to the composing house the task of substituting codes. All that is required is a distinct code for every place in the text that will require a typesetting code. The substitution processes, once the specific typesetter is identified, are similar. The important thing to remember is that all routine typesetting code requirements should be anticipated in the generic codes.

THE BASICS

Let us turn our attention, then, to what the editor needs to know about running computers and using software appropriate to the typesetting process. We cannot dwell on basic computer literacy: knowledge of file management systems, word processing, printouts, and backups. None of these things is very difficult, but novices can read manuals or take short courses in these basic skills. It may be reassuring to know that one does not need to know any programming language or anything about wires, ROM, RAM, chips, or boards. It won't hurt to say, however, that the faster the machine (usually measured in megahertz—MHz in the advertisements), the more advanced the processor (indicated by numbers like 386, 486, and 68030 or names like Pentium and Motorola), the greater the amount of internal memory (RAM), the larger and faster the hard disk, why, the faster the programs will run. These characteristics do not affect one's typing speed, but it will make considerable difference when processing large files with a collating or typesetting program.

There are many word processors and little reason why editors should not use whatever one they have become accustomed to. The important thing to keep in mind is that the computer file sent to the computer typesetter must be free of all control characters except carriage returns and line feeds produced by the return key. A word processor that inserts other control characters to indicate such things as double spacing, indentation, superscripts and subscripts, underlining, or font changes creates files that must be stripped before they can be used for typesetting. Some word processors have a "save text only" option for this purpose. The point is that what goes into the typesetter is a file with only two hidden control characters: the carriage return and line feed at the end of each line of input. All typesetting commands, whether for TₑX or some other system, should be visible (i.e., in normal ASCII characters) in the file. A word processor such as PC-WRITE, though capable of formatting commands for printouts, normally saves text as text only and may therefore be thought convenient for editing files that are not to be formatted by the word processor. NOTE BENE offers an option of implementing the formatting commands or making them a visible (ASCII) part of the file. Many word processors offer the option of implementing the formatting commands or providing an ASCII file with formatting codes stripped out altogether. Although editors will gravitate to one word processor or another for any number of reasons, the point is that most word processors can produce the types of files needed for typesetting.

A laser printer that accepts the typesetting codes being used makes it possible to print and proofread everything in the editor's shop in a format equivalent (except in print quality) to that of the composing house. If one uses generic codes, developed for their ease of use, a conversion will be needed before formatted output can be produced. But a generically coded file can be "dumped" to a printer for proofreading; it just won't be pretty. Editors who cannot convert generic codes to those for a formatted output must wait for the composing house to provide proofs. Solutions to this unsatisfactory procedure are simple but might require an editor to learn to use a new word processor or acquire a conversion program tailored to local needs.

One solution, not the best in my opinion, is to use a word processor such as NOTE BENE, which provides the editor with a WYSIWYG (what you see is what you get) formatted text on the screen and printout but also offers a pure ASCII text with all the format codes visible. Such files can be collated and used to produce apparatus files without loss of format markers. And a conversion from NOTE BENE codes to a typesetting system would be relatively simple to effect. The problem with this solution is that NOTE BENE, like all word processors, is limited in the number of options it offers (what you see is *all* you get). Full-scale typesetting allows more fine-tuning and additional opportunities to arrange and enhance text. Codes for these would have to be added at a late stage and require additional proofreading. But it can be done that way.

Editors using TEX or any of the desktop publishing programs will be a step ahead of editors using word processors, for these programs are more sophisticated in the preparation of publications (as opposed to letters, memos, and typescripts). An editor who can send the publisher a printout that looks typeset already will be in greater control of the accuracy and the look of the end product. The portions of a scholarly edition that will be submitted to a copy editor should be double spaced, a form achieved by a single command, whether with a word processor or a typesetting device.

Editors committed to real typesetting for their editions have several ways to go about it. I will outline two, which perhaps represent extremes. The one that requires learning the least also requires depending the most on others. One should weigh the pros and cons of that remark. It is relatively easy to get the director of the composing house that will prepare camera-ready copy to look over the text after it has been marked by the publisher's copy editor and designer. The composer can create a list of codes to use on the particular job. The editor will not have to figure out how the typesetter works or what demands the craft of typesetting places on the typesetter. Its disadvantage is that one must follow directions by rote, and the editor largely forgoes the opportunity to recognize and implement improvements as works progresses. How each code expands into actual typesetting commands for the computer is none of the concern of the editor.[1] Many editors would be grateful for such a system; it lets them concentrate on the literary style and content of the work, leaving the details of book design and format to someone else.

At the opposite pole from this approach is the method I adopted for producing the first edition of this book. It involved learning enough about a particular typesetting program to write or direct the writing of the macros to be used—in this case with TEX typesetting software.[2] And it involved paying attention to the details of page design (judging the amount of white space that should exist between lines [leading], the size of the type, the width and height of the type page, the style and content of the running headlines, and the position and shape of the footnotes).

The first edition of this book[3] was typeset by a laser printer (300dpi) and reproduced by offset printing, but this kind of output is not acceptable for most book production. What printers call camera-ready copy is produced by a photocomposer or high-resolution (1200dpi) laser printer; the output image is printed on photographic paper. Ordinary laser printers, however, produce a very good preliminary page proof, which may be of high enough quality for certain kinds of publication. The third edition was produced at 600dpi.

At the end of the last chapter I suggested that error-free input to a computer-driven commercial-quality composer was a realizable goal. Regardless of how free of error the text may be or how fully and accurately the typesetting codes have been incorporated into the text, fine-tuning will

---

1. This is essentially the system used in producing the second edition of this book (University of Georgia Press, 1986), for, though I had used TEX commands, the press preferred to use its own commercial supplier, who took my computer files, converted the codes to their codes, and typeset the work by a system I knew nothing about.

2. Donald E. Knuth, *The TEXbook* (Reading, Mass.: Addison-Wesley, 1984). TEX is not child's play, but mathematicians and scientists the world over have learned to used it because it manages the full range of mathematic symbols and specialized formula representations, and a great many editors in literature departments have also learned it because it is the only full-scale desktop typesetting program available. Besides, it is a public domain program, thanks to the generosity of its developer.

3. Titled *Scholarly Editing in the Computer Age: Lectures in Theory and Practice,* published by the English Department, Royal Military College, University of New South Wales, Duntroon, Australia, in 1984.

be required during final type composition. This is true whether the editor "composes" his own final typeset output (camera-ready copy) or if some commercial typesetting company uses the editor's computer files to produce the typeset form. I found fine-tuning to be both time-consuming and frustrating, and I did not manage all the fine-tuning that could be achieved with more time or more knowledge of a typesetting system. Orphans (single lines beginning a paragraph at the bottom of a page), widows (single lines ending a paragraph at the top of a page), the juxtaposition of tight and loose lines, and excessive end-of-line hyphenation are other matters that can be resolved at the fine-tuning stage. And, as with any operation that requires attention, things can go wrong.

The approach I used for the Thackeray Edition Project falls somewhere between the easy and the hard way. I first developed a list of the typesetting requirements for the edition insofar as I could foresee them. They fell into three categories: (1) special characters for letters and symbols and combinations that are not on the keyboard, such as accented letters, Greek letters, and digraphs; (2) style and formatting that occurs within the text, such as type font changes for italics, block indentation, lines of poetry that have to maintain line integrity and should not be justified, and salutations and signatures for letters; and (3) style and formatting that were not within the text, such as page size, running headlines, pagination, and title page specifications. Having made a list of all the special effects and symbols I would be using, I developed a two-stroke mnemonic coding system. Since I did not have to be able to do everything that a typesetter can do, my list was not very long. This generic code system is not in the language of any specific typesetting software. It does, however, anticipate the need for distinctive codes at specific points in the texts. When I began the Thackeray edition, I anticipated working with the composing house that would do the typesetting to develop a substitution list that would enable me to replace my generic codes with the specific codes required by the compositor's equipment. In the event, I did it all myself, learning TEX, converting my generic codes and adding formatting to suit my notion of the edition, and fine-tuning the final production. My files were in final proofread form before a composing house ever saw them. The composing house's one service was to run my files through a machine capable of 1200dpi output.

Practically considered, perhaps the most far-reaching ramification of this process is that the publisher can also bring out the text (with or without the textual apparatuses and introductions) in a different format without having to "reset" the type. Of the practical editions available in the

1970s that were based on CEAA-approved scholarly texts, apparently only the Northwestern-Newberry Melville and the Iowa-California Twain paperback editions did not introduce errors.[4] This was because the sheets of the library edition were simply wrapped in paper for the classroom market. Other paperback texts were reset, more or less faithfully, from the established version to fit with the manufacturer's format. With the advent of electronic typesetting, however, once the text is correct it should not have to be rekeyed. The publisher could photo-offset the texts, or, if reformatting to accord with an existing commercial series is desirable, the publisher could use the magnetic file that was used to set the library edition. Thus, one avoids introducing new errors and eliminates the need for multiple proofreadings. Margins, lines per page, type style and size, even hyphenation, are all variables that can be changed by the introduction of a few initial commands telling the typesetting machine what to do about such matters.[5]

---

4. A sample survey of classroom products appeared in "Practical Editions: A Proof Seminar" in *Proof* (1971–73); they include Anderson, Crane, Emerson, Hawthorne, Howells, Irving, Thoreau, and Twain.

5. This was the case when my Norton Critical Edition text of *Vanity Fair* was derived from my full-scale scholarly edition (1989). The files used to typeset the earlier book were updated by changing the formatting parameters, adding explanatory footnotes, moving selected portions of the textual apparatus into footnotes, and adjusting page breaks and illustration locations. The text remained unchanged except in the case of two or three corrections, noted in the Norton edition.

Chapter Fourteen

Electronic Editions

Because electronic publishing is incunabular, energetic, and exciting, it is surrounded by hype, exaggeration, ignorance, and skepticism. Fantastic and disastrous projects have taken over equipment and energy worthy of better causes. The Gutenberg Project, for example, well on its way to provide 100,000 free electronic texts by the year 2000, occupies the time of scores of persons and space on innumerable computers but is the product of abysmal ignorance of the textual condition. Its texts are unreliable, for they are insufficiently proofread, inadequately marked for font and formatting, and they come from who knows where, their sources unrecorded. Its perpetrators apparently believe that any copy of a given title adequately represents the work, that all copies are equally representative of the work and infinitely interchangeable. Texts are assumed to consist of letters and punctuation in a series, regardless of font or format. In order to ensure that texts can be read by anyone anywhere, all formatting, font specifications, and special typographic effects are eliminated. The Gutenberg Project has been criticized and admonished for these fundamental flaws so frequently, with little or no effect on its practice, that one no longer hesitates to declare it a textual junkyard. Valuable and undamaged items can be found in junkyards, but it takes a scavenger to find them.

Far more respectable and incredibly expensive is *The English Poetry Full-Text Database* from Chadwyck-Healey, offering the works of 1,350 pre-1900 poets on compact disks for $41,000–51,000. An editorial board has selected a source text for each poem from among those not in copyright or readily granted by copyright holders. Although no bibliographical or textual notes indicate the relationship between the edition selected for publication and other editions, the published source text of each poem is identified, and apparently the corpus has been carefully proofread. As with most print collections and anthologies, this database homogenizes the typographic and bibliographic look of the poems, thus reducing each poem to its linguistic code.[1] That is nearly inevitable given the primary aims of the collection: to create a collected corpus of English poetry and to make it computer searchable. But, for our purposes, this database pioneers an element of extreme interest, regardless of how simple the project's textual claims may be. This database is encoded with TEI conformant SGML.[2] TEI's purpose is to establish standard usage of the Standard Generalized Markup Language (SGML) for electronic text exchange in the humanities. What this means for *The English Poetry Full-Text Database* is that, regardless of the computer being used to read the database, texts will appear fully formatted, with proper distinctions among type fonts, font sizes, indentations, and leading.[3] The purpose of SGML is to provide a coding system for the distribution of electronic texts that, regardless of output device, will maintain the integrity of the structural features of the edited text.[4]

We see in these two early projects the energy and excitement with which text users have responded to the easiest feature of computerized texts, the one that stands out the most in distinguishing electronic texts from printed ones: the user's ability to search large texts rapidly for words, phrases, and near juxtaposition of words. These capabilities are evident with any electronic text, though an inaccurately input one might defeat the system.

---

1. I do not consider that a criticism of the project, merely a description of it.

2. The Text Encoding Initiative (TEI) is a project sponsored by the Association for Computers and the Humanities, the Association for Library and Linguistic Computing, the Social Science and Humanities Research Council of Canada, and the Association for Computational Linguistics with funding from the National Endowment for the Humanities (NEH), the Commission of European Communities, and the Mellon Foundation.

3. *Leading* is an oddly anachronistic printer's term to use here for the relative amount of space between lines, an effect no longer achieved by inserting lead strips.

4. SGML was designed with a good deal more than the exchange of fully formatted texts in mind. The standardization of a system is what makes coded files portable to other platforms, but SGML was designed to make it possible to identify all aspects of a text for a great many purposes, such as stylistic and linguistic analyses. So, SGML involves identifying the structural features of texts (book, title, contents, chapters, sections, paragraphs, sentences, phrases, words), the generic features of texts (anthology, introduction, poem, stanza, couplet, line), the bibliographic features of source texts (gathering, leaf, page), and any or all other structural hierarchies, such as the structure of argument. Editors do not need to code all these things, but, if they want to do so, there is a standard way to do it that will be accessible to all readers equipped with SGML readers—which comes with the application.

Electronic scholarly editions are concerned with much more than searchable texts. Not only does the scholarly editor bring to electronic publishing all the concerns of textual criticism that occupied us in the first part of this book; they also find in the electronic medium opportunities to extend their notions of what constitutes the work of art and how it can be read. The TEI/SGML encoding system addresses, in the electronic world, the same fundamental issues of formatting and distribution that typesetting codes address in the print world. Like typesetting codes, SGML codes are developed and implemented best by persons who understand the intricacies of textual existence, who care about the details of presentation as practical problems.[5]

It may not be surprising, therefore, that editors already burdened with the details of textual histories and ambiguous and otherwise mysterious questions of authority should initially consider the opportunities of electronic publishing and the complications of SGML with sinking hearts. Perhaps the first step in realizing the importance of a universal marking system is to say that, without one, an editor developing an electronic edition in, for example, HyperCard on a Macintosh or in ToolBook on a DOS machine has by these choices limited his potential users to folks with a Macintosh of their own or a DOS machine during the years before these machines become obsolete. But the editor with a universal encoding system developing an electronic edition with a multiplatform application has created a tool available to anyone with a computer and has ensured the longevity of the editorial work through generations to come of software and hardware. It seems worth the effort.

But, before trying to lift anyone's spirits about the details, we should, perhaps, contemplate the general outlines of electronic text capabilities and their relation to theories of the text. In addition to providing searchable texts, thus enhancing our sense and grasp of the intratextuality of a work, the electronic medium provides an environment in which the relations between multiple versions of a text and between a text and its verbal, intellectual, and visual parallels can also become more immediate.[6] Of course, inter- and intratextuality have already been available to us in print editions; what is new is the dexterity with which we can explore the relations within

---

5. Again, though it may not be at the top of a scholarly editor's priority list, SGML codes can be used to mark a much larger range of textual features than a typesetting program can, including linguistic and generic categories.

6. This idea is elaborated usefully in Jerome J. McGann's "The Rationale of HyperText" (available on World Wide Web: http://jefferson.village.virginia.edu/generalpubs.html

and between texts for ourselves and the ease and elegance with which editors can lay them out for edition users in electronic form.

A corollary may explain why electronic textuality is so often seen as a revolution equal to that initiated by the invention of printing and movable type. The traditional concept that textuality is linear—that narration, argument, and even rant begins and proceeds and arrives at a conclusion in a traceable if not always predetermined manner, one word after another in an unchanging order for every reader—need not dominate the user's experience of electronic editions. It is true that printed books, particularly reference books and other "machines of knowledge" (McGann's phrase), have been accessible to us in "nonlinear" ways, such as alphabetical entries to be searched by topic headings, as glosses and annotations to be read in tandem with primary texts, and as compendiums, whose main access is through indexes or analytical tables of contents. Nevertheless, the electronic media is often touted as a vehicle for the arrangement of information in a fashion more closely related to the arrangement of information in the mind, where great leaps and sudden bridges juxtapose and unite the unexpected.[7] The compilers of hypertext archives of texts, images, annotations, and perhaps sounds, motions, and smells are not creating intricate mazes through which readers must wander, stymied at the wrong turns before emerging victorious at the designated exits. They are, instead, creating networks of texts in which the prearranged links can be ignored and superseded at any moment for purposes and with results not under the editors' control. And yet the conventional reader can choose to read hypertexts linearly, as of old. The electronic medium has extended the textual world; it has not overthrown books nor the discipline of concentrated "lines" of thought; it has added dimensions and ease of mobility to our concepts of textuality.[8] It follows that electronic scholarly editions are not just print editions available in electronic form. There is nothing to prevent anyone from putting a book text in electronic form, but it seems a waste of a resource to do so.

---

7. See Jerome McGann, "The Complete Writings and Pictures of Dante Gabriel Rossetti: A Hyper Media Research Archive," *Text* 7 (1995): 95–105; Murray McGillvray, "Towards a Post-Critical Editions: Theory, Hypertext, and the Presentation of Middle English Works," *Text* 7 (1994): 175–99; and "Nonlinearity" in *Hyper/Text/Theory*, ed. George Landow (Johns Hopkins University Press, 1994), 51–222—particularly Gunnar Liestrøl, "Wittenstein, Genette, and the Reader's Narrative in Hypertext"; and J. Yellowlees Douglas, "'How Do I Stop This Thing?': Closure and Indeterminacy in Interactive Narratives."

8. These ideas are elaborated in my article "Polymorphic, Polysemic, Protean, Reliable, Electronic Texts," in *Palimpsest: Editorial Theory and the Humanities*, ed. George Bornstein and Ralph G. Williams (Ann Arbor: University of Michigan Press, 1993), 29–43. See also Landow, *Hyper/Text/Theory*.

One vision of an electronic scholarly edition is that the multiplicity of textual forms no longer need to be merely described or represented in a reduced apparatus. Each historically important or authoritative text can be represented in full. This is because of the enormous (and increasing) data storage capacity of compact disks (CD-ROM). Furthermore, the basic research source materials—manuscripts, first editions, correspondence—can be represented both as text (searchable and quotable) and as image (reproducing the appearance of the original), though not both in the same computer file. Sound and motion picture recordings are also feasible aspects of what has become known more as the electronic archive than the electronic edition.

From the point of view of the bibliographic, documentary, and sociological orientations, the electronic archive may itself represent the editorial goal: each historical document represented in full without editing, without the mediating intervention of an editor trying to represent in small space the features and characteristics of unique or rare originals. Instead, full texts and full images are made manifest. Editors in search of self-effacement and objectivity may believe they have found in the electronic archive the perfect medium for unobtrusive editorial service. Yet, a "mere" archive of source materials will strike most new readers and researchers from other fields as an undigested chaos of material in which everyone must become an editor before proceeding. The electronic archive can (some would say must) provide more than access to source materials.

A second vision of the electronic scholarly edition or archive is of one webbed or networked with cross-references connecting variant texts, explanatory notes, contextual materials, and parallel texts. An archive in a hypertext environment can provide radiating access routes to all its parts. The electronic edition is not primarily, then, a place to sit and read through a novel or poem for a first-time experience of the work or for the pleasure of a good read. It is a tool for students of a work, returning to it with the intention of exploring its history, its connective tissues, its roots and ramifications. Such students want to be able to search texts from stem to stern electronically, to move directly from one passage in a work to its corresponding passages in other versions or from a text to its sources or contexts in other works. They want annotations, textual variants, variorums of critical commentaries, dramatizations, and film and TV versions available from the archive at the click of a "hot spot" in the text before them. They want textual and historical accounts of composition and publication.

Editors and readers of the authorial orientation will not be content with a webbed, introduced, and annotated array of existing authoritative texts, for they have found repeatedly the fact that authorial intentions have been thwarted, distorted, vitiated, or maybe just slightly but irritatingly altered in the production process. Their textual research repeatedly shows that manuscripts fail to represent the full intention for the work and that printed texts repeatedly fail to fulfill the author's expectations. In short, they find that an archive of existing texts is an archive of texts rendered unsatisfactory by typos, omissions, additions, conflations, compromises, and ineptitudes. Unlike sociological editors, who find in these the texture of social, economic, and artistic exchanges, authorial editors are unwilling to resign themselves to the notion that whatever is, is right. They will, in the electronic edition as in the print edition, provide an edited, critical, eclectic text representing their notion of what the text should have been—the new text webbed and cross-referenced into the archive as was never possible in the print world. Readers disdaining the eclectic text need but to ignore it, concentrating on other parts of the archive.

The beauty of full-scale, scholarly electronic editions is that students of a text will more readily than was ever the case in print editions be able to confront textual cruxes for themselves, not merely or even primarily in order to second-guess the editor but, rather, in order to explore the critical implications to their own uses of the text. And this is to say nothing of the added freedom to annotate at various levels of detail in hypertext environments.

PRACTICALITIES

In order to achieve a workable, distributable, usable electronic edition, an editor needs a system for *encoding the texts* so that persons operating different computer machines will still be able to read the archive without loss of textual information or the links between related parts of the archive and so that, when advances in technology make the current hardware and software obsolete, the textual work can be preserved, enhanced, and transported to new and better systems. The editor also needs a *hypertext authoring program* with which to create the archive (and each user will need to be supplied with a reader's version designed to work with the specific computer's operating system). And the editor needs a *distribution medium* in which the archive can reach potential users or through which users can reach it. At the moment this last requirement is a choice among tape, compact disk, or Internet access. But there is little point here in specifying software or hardware except as examples of practical solutions, for best choices are constantly being superseded.

Text encoding is not a trivial matter. At a very basic level people have been exchanging texts across computer platforms[9] and between software text handlers in the universal character code known as ASCII, but in that exchange mode all formatting and font indications are lost or exist only as codes. This is the case not only for transfers of text from one operating system to another, but, even within an operating system, different software packages, particularly word processors and spreadsheets, encode files with proprietary coding systems. So, transfer of files from one software package to another also requires conversion to ASCII text. Some conversion packages (sometimes called bridges or black boxes) are designed to take a file fully coded for one specific package and convert it to a file fully coded for another in a process that is transparent to the user. But these limitations on the exchange of files mean either we must dispense with formatting and fonts or we must stick to exchanges between specified programs for which conversion programs have been made or we must have a system that universalizes font and formatting features as well as letters, spaces, and punctuation.

One solution, developed with print world mentality, is the extraordinarily successful and versatile *Postscript* language, which allows a Postscript-encoded text to be printed out in nearly identical format on nearly any printer running any one of many postscript compatible print programs. Postscript files are, however, useless in their electronic form for any purpose other than to convey a formatted text to a printer or to a screen viewer; they are not searchable or quotable. So, they won't do for our purposes.

Another solution, developed with worldwide electronic access in mind is HTML, an encoding system that is highly flexible and that currently has the advantage over every competitor that it is almost universally accessible on the Internet for use in a hypertext environment known as World Wide Web (WWW). Its deficiencies are that it does not allow specification of every detail that scholarly editors find significant to report or to keep track of and that its flexibility allows too much internal variation in the way it represents items that it does record. The result of this second flaw is that different end users accessing the archive may see different visual representations of the same text: fonts and formats are too flexible.

The most promising solution at the moment is *TEI-conformant SGML*, designed to ensure that a file uploaded from the originator's hard and software environment is duplicated when the material is downloaded into a

---

9. A platform is any computer running a particular operating system such as DOS, UNIX, or Macintosh.

different hardware and software environment. Parsers (software to automate the uploading and downloading) are proliferating. *Guidelines for Electronic Text Encoding and Interchange (TEI P3)*, edited by C. M. Sperberg-McQueen and Lou Burnard, is the manual for the encoding system, inviting even the timid with its second chapter, "A Gentle Introduction to SGML."[10]

Sharing across platforms texts that carry the full complement of textual signifiers is only the beginning. Hypertext linking of texts to other texts or to other parts of itself or to annotations is achieved within specific hypertext and multimedia software packages, each in some way different from other software that might be used. And most hypertext authoring and reading systems are platform specific. Editors need to be able to provide editions in a medium that is not "platform specific" if the goal is to create electronic scholarly editions that can be used by anybody anywhere, regardless of the type of computer. It helps to look at this large problem in parts: authoring a hypertext archive, distributing a hypertext application on a compact disk, and making a hypertext archive available on the net.

A helpful distinction to make is between authoring and reading a hypertext application. Read-only programs can be simple and free, distributed with applications as part of the package. Authoring programs are complex and expensive. The important point is to "author" one's edition in a software package (1) that has compatible reader programs for each of the major operating platforms and (2) that accepts and handles TEI-conformant SGML texts.[11] Regardless of the specific machine on which the editor is authoring the electronic archive, the result of the work will be readable by any user with the appropriate (free) reader software.

The next issue concerns a medium of delivery. At the moment compact disks seem to be the medium of choice for book publishers entering the electronic edition market. Compact disks, CDs, are cheaper to manufacture than books, and they can be packaged, distributed, and sold like

---

10. TEI has an ongoing electronic list for discussion of questions and developments. (Send a message to listserv@uicvm.uic.edu that says: subscribe TEI-L <your name>.) Backlogs of discussion are available. Regularly updated versions of TEI DTDs (document type definitions) are posted at ftp-tei.uci.edu and ftp.ex.ac.uk. Other helps are available on World Wide Web (e.g., http://www.oclc.org/fred/ *and* http://www.sil.org/sgml/sgml.html).

11. That sentence comes perilously close to being an endorsement of TEI, but any system that effects universal delivery of fully marked texts protecting the integrity of editorial work would do as well. I know of no such system other than TEI at this time. Likewise, I know of no authoring program other than DynaText at this time that accepts SGML marked files and has readers for the three major operating platforms. It is more likely that other appropriate multiplatform authoring programs will be developed than that SGML will have a viable competitor.

books. Because all the text matter in the edition is in ASCII, marked by universal codes, users need only be sure to get the version with the appropriate reader software for their particular computer. The CD medium allows publishers to operate with nearly the same marketing techniques and distribution systems they use for books.

Reflection suggests, however, that there are serious problems with the idea of making CDs the primary mode of existence or the end product of electronic editing—the goal determining the standards of data capture and storage. One problem is the need to create multiple forms of each CD for different platforms, which involves duplication of effort for each archive created. Another is that, once distributed, any further improvements to the archive would either be forgone by previous purchasers or new editions would need to be distributed. A third is that it requires that each user's computer be big enough to house sophisticated multimedia software as well as the whole archive in order to have maximum utility.

Furthermore, an editor who has compiled the source materials, edited them, provided all the needed marking, and supplied the hypertext links within the archive may wonder what added value is supplied by a publisher. There is the Internet, after all, accessible freely to the world of internet users. Many editors are connected to institutions whose computing center can offer a home page for the archive on the World Wide Web. WWW, with hypertext systems such as Mosaic and Netscape, employ HTML coding for texts and have reader software for all three major operating platforms.[12] WWW provides access to archives and data banks on the Internet and reads texts, displays digital images, and activates the links that form the hypertext web. This is accomplished by downloading significant portions to the user's hard disk or printer. Even with fast equipment, this process will seem slow at times. A better solution might be to allow distance users from *their* home computers to operate the networked application on *its* home computer.[13]

As of this writing, there has been no hypertext software developed designed specifically for developing electronic scholarly editions. The most

---

12. It is only fair to point out that the glories of Mosaic or Netscape and WWW, like the glories of any hypertext application accessing huge amounts of textual or visual data, requires fast processors, high-resolution screens, large hard disks, and sophisticated printers for satisfactory results. Furthermore, WWW and Mosaic or Netscape are limited to HTML, not SGML marking, though downloaded SGML files can then be viewed with a parser like Panorama.

13. As traffic on the internet thickens, there have been frequent interruptions and failures in long-distant access, which will probably be addressed by the next wave of internet hardware.

promising package to date, DynaText, does provide multiple windows with parallel scrolling of linked texts, and it does use SGML-marked texts intelligently. It is not a strong multi-media package, however, and it does not have a built in collating or automatic variant text linking capability. MAC-CASE does have collating and automatic variant text linking but has no multimedia or automatic SGML-marking capability. COLLATE has add-on software to automate part of the SGML-marking process but is not a hypertext or multimedia authoring package. In short, scholarly editors are to the point where just about everything they would like to do with computers in research or text preparation or text presentation is implemented in one set of software or another, but no package of programs has been coordinated to unite rationally all the desired element.

Once we find or develop the adequate authoring software and navigational software—adequate in the sense that it lets us do all the things that users of scholarly electronic editions want to do—then the *archive* version of the software and the *user* versions of the software can be coordinated: users will have software resident at their personal work stations, the network will connect them to the archive or database in its home environment, and the database version of the software will navigate the archive. It is *access* to the editions rather than the *editions* themselves that need to be platform independent.

Turning briefly to the painful details, the editor who cares deeply about the minutiae of the textual condition and who has already braved the intricacies of typesetting codes may yet have the intricacies of TEI-conformant SGML codes to learn. It will someday, perhaps already, be the case, as it was in the "print world," that coding-service agencies will develop. In the print world they are called compositors and typesetters—who take paper copy marked in pencil by the copy editor and produce professionally typeset camera-ready copy. In that world the editor had a large proofreading assignment but did not need to learn codes. So, service bureaus, the compositors of electronic editions, will emerge, taking computer files and hard copy marked to indicate the editor's wishes and encode them for electronic distribution. Again, it may be that the editor will not have to learn SGML or any other system but will choose, instead, a major proofreading assignment. In the short run, however, and while the conventional shapes of electronic scholarly editions are still being invented and discovered, at least some editors will want the kind of control over the electronic appearance of their work that can only be had by doing the work themselves.

As with typesetting, one needs to learn the basic principles and intricacies of that part of the coding system that applies to the project at hand.

Unlike a professional compositor, who must know the system well enough to handle every job that comes in the door, the scholarly editor has but one customer and one limited set of demands to meet. But one must know the system well enough to provide elegant, rather than "cludged," solutions to each problem. A novice must seek out manuals, courses, electronic bulletin boards, discussion lists, and knowledgeable friends for help.

But a thought to alleviate some of the pain, and one that will be useful even to editors unwilling to travel this third mile: the in-house, generic coding that computer age editors included as part of the original input in order to keep track of the font and formatting features of the source texts, and which were used as the basis for conversion to typesetting codes, remain now to be used as the basis for initial conversion to SGML codes. As with typesetting, the more precisely and fully the text files were coded to begin with, the easier the conversion becomes for typesetting and for electronic presentation. The principle is hard but simple: the editor who hopes always to keep things as simple as possible will travel many blind alleys; the editor who from the beginning of the project has foreseen the range of uses and presentation systems for the finished work will save time and money and gain greater control over the quality of end products.

Glossary

This glossary is provided as an extension and summary of definitions for terms that have been used in the profession to mean any number of different things. It is not a comprehensive glossary of editorial terms, nor does it attempt to give the most common or standard "textbook" definitions.

authorial. Originating with the author.

authoritative. Having or representing the sanction of or the power of *authority*. Not to be confused with *authorial*.

authority. The person, persons, or conceptual or institutional framework that has the right to generate or alter *text* for the *work of art*. Not to be confused with *author*.

collaboration. The act of sharing *authority* over a *work* or some portion of it.

copy-text. The text that is the basis for the edited text. Copy-text readings are adopted by the editor unless some cause exists to change them, in which case the editor emends. The copy-text is usually the text found in one document, but that is not always the case.

  setting copy. Known to bibliographers and historians of printing as *printer's copy*, the setting copy is the document or documents from which a compositor sets the text for a printed edition. The terms *printer's copy* and *copy-text* are sometimes confused, but the former is a *document* (physical object) and the latter is a *text* (sequence of words and punctuation).

definitive. The Holy Grail of editing—an unattainable object of quest; all the crusaders have gone home.

definitive text. A term used primarily in the 1960s to describe the products of scholarly editing when appealing for funding on the grounds that the work once done definitively would never have to be done again.

definitive edition. A descriptive term that reached prominence in the 1970s to replace *definitive text*. It was meant to indicate that, taken as a whole—text and apparatus—a scholarly edition could represent definitive research that would never have to be done again, though the text itself might be re-edited according to differing principles.

diplomatic transcription. A rendering in machine-produced form (typing or typeset) of the entire content of a manuscript, marked proof, or annotated text, including cancellations and additions. One can think of a diplomatic transcription as a *genetic text* limited to the record of composition available in the document being transcribed. There are many conventions for producing diplomatic transcriptions.

record of manuscript alterations. These records are usually meant to serve the same purpose as the diplomatic transcription. Several methods have been devised, including reprinting the altered portions as they would appear in a diplomatic transcription or giving verbal descriptions of the alterations.

document. The physical vessel (such as a book, manuscript, phonograph record, computer tape) that contains (or incarnates) the *text*. See also chap. 4.

text. The sequence of words and pauses recorded in a *document*.

source text. The earliest document containing any given textual feature.

edited text. The sequence of words and punctuation produced when a nonauthoritative agent (such as a scholar) attempts to make a text more correct or more purely authoritative by following some editorial principle.

corrupt text. A text produced carelessly, containing *typographical errors* and demonstrably nonauthoritative and inferior readings.

sophisticated text. A text purporting to be a faithful copy but containing introduced variants that are syntactically plausible. The sophistications may or may not be "improvements" but, on the whole, are considered to have been produced according to faulty editorial principles. *Sophisticated texts* are *corrupt texts,* though not all corrupt texts are sophisticated.

critical text. Any edited text that results from the application of rationally defensible editorial principles. One could say that a documentary edition that produces an edited text that is textually identical with its source text is a critical text because its text was chosen on some critical basis over any alternative authoritative source text. That is, however, a wasteful and potentially misleading use of the term. See chap. 8.

genetic text. A text revealing the development of authoritative forms of the work. An operative definition of *authority* is necessary to determine what a genetic text will or should include. For example, a genetic text that includes all variants from all documents in the development of a work is implementing a documentary definition of authority. A genetic text, on the other hand, that implements an authorial definition of *authority* will omit from the record of genesis any textual material that did not originate with or receive the sanction of the author, unless such nonauthoritative matters impinged upon the author's consciousness, influencing other alterations that the author did make.

textual transmission. The reproduction of texts from one document to another. Transmission need not involve variation; a text can be accurately reproduced. It may be transmitted by an authoritative or nonauthoritative agent. Understanding textual transmission involves identifying textual alterations and all the circumstances influencing their production and reproduction. Study of textual transmission is crucial in determining the authority of alterations. When an alteration cannot be attributed to a specific agency in the textual transmission, it is said to be an *indifferent variant*. Whether a transmitting agent is authoritative or nonauthoritative will depend on the definition being used for authority. See also chaps. 1 and 7.

typographical error. A reading (which may or may not be variant) that is so implausible as to admit of no other explanation for its existence than that it occurred accidentally when the author (or scribe or compositor) was trying to produce a different reading.

variant. An alteration in a text. Variants can be *authoritative* (belonging to the work), nonauthoritative (unfortunately imposed on the work), or *indifferent* (not certainly authoritative or nonauthoritative).

    indifferent variant. An alteration that cannot with certainty be attributed to a specific originating transmitting agent and therefore cannot be known with certainty to be authoritative or nonauthoritative.

version. One of two or more authoritative forms of a *work*. There may be disagreement over whether or not a variant reading or collection of variant readings constitutes any unity of effect that demands significant critical attention. See also chap. 4.

work. The message or experience implied by the authoritative versions of a literary writing. Usually the variant forms have the same name. Sometimes there will be disagreement over whether a variant form is in fact a variant *version* or a separate work.

Suggested Readings

BIBLIOGRAPHIES

The Center for Scholarly Editions: An Introductory Statement New York: Modern Language Association, 1977. (With "A Third Interim Supplement [1992]," by G. Thomas Tanselle; additional supplements scheduled). Note: This selective list of basic readings in post-Medieval textual studies is comprehensive enough to keep the most ardent student busy a very long time. Available from the MLA's Committee on Scholarly Editions, MLA, 10 Astor Place, New York, NY 10003-6981.

Greetham, David. "Selected Bibliography," *Textual Scholarship: An Introduction*. New York: Garland Publishing, 1994, pp. 419–526. Note: This equally daunting list is arranged according to sub-fields of Textual Scholarship, from ennumerative to descriptive bibliography, from paleography to typography, and from textual criticism to scholarly editing. Many items appear in more than one section.

———, ed. *Scholarly Editing: A Guide to Research* New York: Modern Language Association, 1995. Contains bibliographical essays on varieties of scholarly editing and on special fields from biblical and classical, through all periods of English and American literature, to several foreign literatures and folk literature.

WORLD WIDE WEB PAGES

British Poetry 1780–1910: a Hypertext Archive of Scholarly Editions
http://www.lib.virginia.edu/etext/britpo/html

General Publications of the Institute of Advanced Technologies in the Humanities
http://jefferson.village.edu/generalpubs.html
Includes essays by Hoyt Duggan, Jerome McGann, and John Unsworth and links to the Rossetti Archive.

JOURNALS AND SPECIAL ISSUES

[Special issue on Editing], *Romance Philology* 45, no. 1 (1991).
Editing and the Imagination Special Number, *Studies in the Literary Imagination* 29, no. 1 (1996).
Textual Studies in the Novel Special Number, *Studies in the Novel*, 7, no. 3 (1975).
Editing Novels and Novelists, Now Special Number, *Studies in the Novel*, 27, 3 (1995).
Text: Transactions of the Society for Textual Scholarship/ 1– ; (1984–).

BOOKS AND CONFERENCE PROCEEDINGS

Contemporary German Editorial Theory. Hans Walter Gabler, George Bornstein, and Gillian Borland Pierce, eds. Ann Arbor: University of Michigan Press, 1995.
Devils and Angels. Phil Cohen, ed. Charlottesville: University Press of Virginia, 1991.
Editing D.H. Lawrence: New Versions of a Modern Author. Charles L. Ross and Dennis Jackson, eds. Ann Arbor: University of Michigan Press, 1995.
Editing in Australia. Paul Eggert, ed. Canberra: English Department, University of New South Wales, University College, ADFA, 1990.
Greetham, D. C. *Textual Scholarship: An Introduction*. New York: Garland, 1992; rev. 1994.
———. *Theories of the Text*. Oxford: Oxford University Press. Forthcoming, 1996.
Grigely, Joseph. *Textualterity: Art, Theory, and Textual Criticism*. Ann Arbor: University of Michigan Press, 1995.
The Literary Text in the Digital Age. Richard J. Finneran, ed. Ann Arbor: University of Michigan Press, 1996.
Machan, Tim William. *Textual Criticism and Middle English Texts*. Charlottesville: University Press of Virginia, 1994.
McGann, Jerome J. *A Critique of Modern Textual Criticism*. Chicago: University of Chicago Press, 1983.

————. *The Textual Condition*. Princeton: Princeton University Press, 1991.

Mailloux, Steven. *Interpretive Conventions: The Reader in the Study of American Fiction*. Ithaca: Cornell University Press, 1982.

New Directions in Textual Studies. Dave Oliphant and Robin Bradford, eds. Austin, Texas: Harry Ransom Humanities Research Center, 1990.

Palimpsest: Editorial Theory in the Humanities. George Bornstein and Ralph Williams, eds. Ann Arbor: University of Michigan Press, 1993

Reiman, Donald H. *The Study of Modern Manuscripts*. Baltimore: Johns Hopkins University Press, 1993.

Representing Modernist Texts: Editing as Interpretation. George Bornstein, ed. Ann Arbor: University of Michigan Press, 1991.

Stillinger, *Multiple Authorship and the Myth of Solitary Genius*. Oxford: Oxford University Press, 1991.

————. *Coleridge & Textual Instability* Oxford: Oxford University Press, 1994.

Tanselle, G. Thomas. *A Rationale of Textual Criticism*. Philadelphia: University of Pennsylvania Press, 1989.

Textual Criticism and Literary Interpretation. Jerome J. McGann, ed. Chicago: University of Chicago Press, 1985.

ARTICLES

Eggert, Paul. "Document and Text: The 'Life' of the Literary Work and the Capacities of Editing." *Text* 7 (1994): 1–24.

Eggert, Paul. "Textual Product or Textual Process: Procedures and Assumptions of Critical Editing" in *Editing in Australia*: 19–40; rept. in *Devils and Angels*: 57–77.

Gorman, David. "The Worldy Text: Writing as Social Action, Reading as Historical Reconstruction." *Literary Theory's Future*. Joseph Natoli, ed. Urbana: University of Illinois Press, 1989: 181–220.

Greetham, D. C. "A Suspicion of Texts." *Thesis* 2, no. 1 (Fall, 1987): 18–25. This was a talk to entering graduate students, interesting, general, inspirational, but revealing DCG's real interests in the problems of textuality.

————. "Editorial and Critical Theory: From Modernism to Post-Modernism" in *Palimpsest*: 9–28.

————. "Politics and Ideology in Current Anglo-American Textual Scholarship." *Editio* 4 (1990): 1–20.

———. "Textual and Literary Theory: Redrawing the Matrix." *Studies in Bibliography* 42 (1989): 1–24.

———. "[Textual] Criticism and Deconstruction." *Studies in Bibliography* 44 (1991): 1–30.

———. "Textual Scholarship." *Introduction to Literary Scholarship in the Modern Languages and Literatures.* Joseph Gibaldi, ed. New York: MLA. 2nd ed. 1992: 103–37.

Groden, Michael. "Contemporary Textual and Literary Theory" in *Representing Modernist Texts: Editing as Interpretation*: 259–86.

McGann, Jerome J. "Interpretation, Meaning, and Textual Criticism: A Homily." *Text* 3 (1987): 55–62.

———. "What Is Critical Editing?" *Text* 5 (1991): 15–30.

———. "Theories of Texts." *London Review of Books* 18 Feb. 1988: 20–21.

McLaverty, James. "The Concept of Authorial Intention in Textual Criticism." *The Library,* sixth ser. (June 1984): 121–38.

———. "The Mode of Existence of Literary Works of Art: The Case of the *Dunciad* Variorum." *Studies in Bibliography* 37 (1984): 82–105.

McLeod, Randall. "Information upon Information." *Text* 5 (1991): 241–86.

Pearsall, Derek. "Editing Medieval Texts." *Textual Criticism and Literary Interpretation.* Jerome J. McGann, ed. Chicago: University of Chicago Press, 1985: 92–106.

Shillingsburg, Peter. "An Inquiry into the Social Status of Texts and Modes of Textual Criticism." *Studies in Bibliography* 42 (1989): 55–79.

———. "Authorial Autonomy vs Social Contract: The Case of *Henry Esmond*" in *Editing in Australia*: 41–64; rpt. in *Devils and Angels*: 22–43.

———. "The Meaning of the Scholarly Edition." *Bulletin of the Bibliographical Society of Australia and New Zealand* 13 (1990): 41–50.

———. "Text as Matter, Concept, and Action." *Studies in Bibliography* 44 (1991) 31–82.

———. "Textual Angst." *LiNQ* 21 (1994): 71–93.

———. "Textual Variants, Performance Variants, and the Concept of Work." *Bulletin of the Bibliographical Society of Australia and New Zealand* 15 (1991): 60-71; rpt. *Editio* 7 (1993): 221–34.

Tanselle, G. Thomas. "Editing Without a Copy-Text." *Studies in Bibliography* 47 (1994): 1–22.

———. "The Editorial Problem of Final Authorial Intention." *Studies in Bibliography* 29 (1976): 167–211. The most sophisticated analytical treatment of the subject before the influence of poststructuralism.

———. "Textual Criticism and Deconstruction." *Studies in Bibliography* 43 (1990): 1–33.

———. "Textual Criticism and Literary Sociology." *Studies in Bibliography* 44 (1991): 83–143.

———. "Textual Instability and Editorial Idealism," *Studies in Bibliography*, 49 (1996), 1–60.

Index